THE Seeding
MICKI EVRIS

Copyright © 2022 by Michelle Evris. All rights reserved.

All rights reserved. No part of this book may be reproduced or transmitted in any form or by any means, electronic or mechanical, including photocopying, recording, or by any information storage and retrieval system without express written permission from the author, except in the case of brief quotations embodied in critical reviews and certain other noncommercial uses permitted by copyright law.

Published in the United States of America

Brilliant Books Literary
137 Forest Park Lane Thomasville
North Carolina 27360 USA

Contents

Prologue 5

Chapter 1	Time To Get Going	9
Chapter 2	Water Ways	14
Chapter 3	It's Just A Dream	21
Chapter 4	What Are You Doing Here?	28
Chapter 5	The Seeding	33
Chapter 6	The Whole Story	39
Chapter 7	Training The Lilliputians	43
Chapter 8	Recon	54
Chapter 9	The Final Preparation	63
Chapter 10	The Battle	71
Chapter 11	The Homecoming	80

Epilogue: A Readers Companion To The Seeding 85
About The Author 93

PROLOGUE

AT FIRST GLANCE, THIS book may appear to be a children's book, but it is actually intended to address several topics that will take some lengthy contemplation in order to consider the meaning, validity, fact, or fiction of its contents. It is meant to spark a desire to go deeper into the understanding of self, and into the relationship we have with all things existing around us. Hopefully it will, at the very least, bring a new found respect for the little things we all take for granted. Some of the concepts presented are not new, but another way to examine them is offered.

Everything we coexist with, including: solids, liquids, gases, plasmas, animals, vegetables, minerals, and the jalopy we drive to work in, deserves a deeper appreciation for their participation in our life story. All things have atomic or molecular movement, including that jalopy you may or may not have. So, we all share in this wonderful energetic movement called atomic vibration. This vibration may change its rate of motion, yet it still continues on even after physical death. The energy that gives movement to the atom is eternally running through all things.

Because of the vibratory energy link we share with all things, we effect our environment and all things within it in a profound way, as our environment and all things within it affect us. Scientifically, we have observed that when two or more independent vibration or rhythmic processes are in proximity of each other, they may synchronize with each other, this is known as entrainment. This process is happening with all things, from the rhythms of the planets to the cells in our bodies. An example of this was demonstrated by Dutch physicist Christian Huygens, inventor of the pendulum clock. Huygens mounted two pendulum clocks together on a board and found, after a period of time; the pendulums would swing with the same rhythm. This phenomenon can be seen when fireflies in a group begin to flash as one beating light. Thought waves will also interact with the environment creating a push-pull relationship with one another till adjustments are made, usually the weaker vibration will adjust to the dominant vibration. In some cases one vibration will slow while the other speeds up in order to adjust to one another. In other cases, they may not adjust at all and exist in disharmony. At any rate, there is clearly sufficient evidence that a relationship exists energetically between all things.

In quantum entanglement, Einstein called it "spooky action at a distance", we observe that when two or more particles interact with each other, irrespective of distance, a correlation will always exist between them. What effects one particle will always affect the other, no matter how far apart they are separated. As people interact with each other in life, they will remain entangled on a quantum level, no mater how far apart they move from each other. Thus, our personal experiences may not be as personal as we think.

Further insights into the connectivity of all things is seen in the work of Masaru Emoto. He observed that thoughts, words, and sound have an effect on the crystalline pattern formations formed in water. He found that water imprinted with positive words or thoughts had a beautiful symmetrical crystalline form, while negative words or thoughts create an asymmetrical unappealing blob-like shape. Since our physical bodies are composed of about 70% water, imagine the effects our thoughts, words, and emotions have on our physical well being.

THE SEEDING

The idea of water having a memory was examined and brought to public attention by French scientist Jacques Benveniste. In his discovery, he diluted an allergenic substance over and over until nothing was left but water. Even though the water was diluted to the point of having no allergenic substances left within it, the purified water still caused an allergic reaction when added to living cells. The French virologist and Nobel Prize Winner, Luc Montognier stated, "What we have found is that DNA produces structural changes in water, which persists at very high dilutions, and which lead to resonant electromagnetic signals that we can measure." It seems an energetic imprint is retained by the water, effecting whatever it may come in contact with next.

These discoveries invite the questions as to: What kind of imprint are we leaving on our environment with our thought, sounds, and vibrations? If we are prone to be of a dominant energy, is it one that can be harmoniously entrained or will it bring disharmony, or even entrain destruction? How will our future actions affect our past relationships through entanglement?

The story you are about to read is a pleasant, and at times humorous fiction with a ribbon of truth running through it. The connectivity among the fabric of animate or inanimate vitalities, the impact of water imprinted with the knowledge of constructive or destructive qualities, and the effect our thoughts, words, and actions have on the structure of creation, are the magic to be discovered within the pages of this book. The principles expressed work well for me in my life experience, try them on or just enjoy the story.

At the conclusion, you will find an epilogue detailing a practical application of the principles conveyed in the story.

CHAPTER 1

TIME TO GET GOING

MICKI EVRIS

A NEW ACADEMIC SEASON ROLLS in for the recruits at The Wolff Academy for Gifted Children. Only a few select children are chosen every six years to attend this prestigious school. The students are selected by their leadership qualities, intuitive skills, and ability to adapt quickly to unusual stimulus.

Alarms go off while parents coax their children out of bed to prepare for the dawn of magnificent wonders that only the Wolff Academy can offer.

"Wake up Jr., it's time for school. I have to get to work. I'll see you later. Have a good day at the academy and don't forget to do the dishes," Jr's. mother directed as she kissed him goodby on the forehead and headed out the door.

Jr. Fishman, a 12 year old long and lanky sprout with a pretty boy face and oversized feet, has his mothers curly red hair, milky smooth skin, and tender heart blended with his fathers athletic prowess and wild, reckless imagination. Every thing Jr. does is in hyperdrive. The only thing Jr. slows down for is Melissa Clark, his sixth grade sweeten-treat. She is his kitten, his inamorata, and he is her Pepe Le Pew. Of course, the universe saw it fitting that Melissa and Jr. be fated to attend the Wolff Academy together.

With the skill of a pole vaulter, Jr. elevated the entire lower half of his body off the bed and catapulted himself to a safe landing onto the worn wooden floor now beneath his cold feet. Nearly airborne, he flash fired himself into the bathroom and splashed cold water on his face and into his mouth, now sufficiently cleaned, by Jr.'s standards. In one smooth and nimble maneuver, Jr. leaped from stair one to the bottom landing to get something that resembled nourishment down his throat for breakfast. A piece of three-day-

THE SEEDING

old, half eaten pizza and a glass of whatever was on the counter from last night would appease the hunger monster. "Oh my Gosh, I'm gonna be late!", he said, now grimacing from the water paint he just swallowed. Jr. dropped his glass on top the mound of yesterday's dishes and dashed out the door, skillfully neglecting clean-up duty he was assigned to do by his beautiful hard working mother, Bridgett Fishman.

Jr. was well on his way to his first lesson in "life dimensions" with Professor Clarence Spalding, a well known metaphysician with a prodigious expertise in the laws governing universal inter dimensional relationships with man. Jr. has a generous imagination and has a tendency for getting sidetracked, which usually ends up making him late for just about everything, including his first day of class.

Jr. jumped up to snap a branch off an unsuspecting oak tree residing on the side of the dirt road he is dashing down. Swatting at the air with his newly acquired weapon, Jr. spots a mud puddle and bounded straight for it. Spattering mud on his new khaki pants upon touch down he growled, "take that you lackey! I am the Lord of this forest and you shall do my bidding!" Thrusting the gnarled limb repeatedly in front of his lanky body while making his way to the rose bush just ahead Jr. shouts, "and for you, you dirty scoundrel, I shall skewer your head in two."

Melissa Clark spotted Jr. acting like his usual goofy boy self on the road ahead of her. "You're gonna be late Jr. Fishman and your moms gonna kill you. You're such a goofy boy," she said. Jr. dropped his weapon and slipped into high gear. Jr exuberantly shouted, "oh man, oh man, oh man, I hope professor Spalding is a nice guy and cuts me some slack. I'll see you later Mel." Jr. kicked it up another notch leaving a cloud of dust behind his whirling feet.

Melissa's long curly blond hair trailed behind her as she skillfully manipulated her bicycle around the potholes in the road. She painstakingly avoided the muddy water accumulated in the pot holes as not to soil her lavender skirt with matching beret. There wasn't a day that went by that Melissa didn't sport a splash of lavender in her apparel along with a matching back pack to complete the ensemble. There is a short cut to Professor Spalding's lab that Melissa found and used today specifically to beat Jr. on the way to class. "I just love to frazzle that boy," Melissa triumphantly declared. Melissa had a feeling this course was going to change her life for the best and wouldn't be late for anything. Just as planned, Melissa was the first to arrive in the classroom, and couldn't wait to see Mr. Speedy Pants Fishman's face when he sees she beat him there.

Arron Glassman, Jr.'s right hand man, is always prepared and suitably attired for class at least an hour in advance. Arron would never consider leaving the house without freshly polished penny-loafers, a starched white shirt, and a befitting power tie. A very proper boy with a strict German upbringing. Every action Arron takes is well thought out with several options carefully considered.

The Glassman home is much like boot camp in the military with spit shined shoes, and morning inspections. The pungent odor of ammonia filled the air from daily floor sterilizations. Mrs. Glassman, like a drill sergeant, keeps the family on their toes shouting a multitude of orders to Arron and her husband Adam.

"Come here Arron, let's have a look at you!" Mrs Glassman commanded. Arron's mother adjusted his tie and spit shined his face with the handkerchief she keeps tucked away between her grapefruit size breasts just for occasions such as this. Mrs Glassman, with her compelling, robust stature and booming vociferations, runs a tight ship with little room for untidiness or disorganization. "Your father is bringing the car around to collect you, are you sufficiently prepared to go?", Arron's mother inquired. "Yes Momma, just have to get my glasses," Arron respectfully replied. Arron briskly walked to his bedroom to collect his spectacles and take inventory of his school supplies as not to forget anything. One last glance in the mirror to run a comb through his slicked back hair should cover all the bases, Arron appraised. Arron gave his mother a peck on the cheek and worked his way to the back seat of his fathers Cadillac. "Ok Poppa, everything is copacetic and I'm ready to go," Arron stated.

Arron's father released the parking brake and carefully manipulated his newly acquired automobile onto the road. "Have you there in a jiffy boy. Are you nervous?", Arron's father asked. "No sir, I am sufficiently prepared," Arron replied. As calculated, Arron arrived precisely on the button to his lesson.

CHAPTER 2

WATER WAYS

THE SEEDING

*T*HE WOLFF ACADEMY FOR Gifted Children is an old, three story cathedral with three arched entrance ways holding mammoth oak doors to accommodate its assemblage. Long looming hallways amplify every whisper keeping nothing a secret. People have been known to vanish into the bowels of the cathedral never to be seen again, at least it's rumored to be so. The faculty voted to keep the classrooms sparsely filled to around ten to twelve students per room to provide a more focused education. The large rooms tend to be cold and damp due to stone walls, lack of insulation, and low level of group body heat.

Professor Spalding's lab is much the same as the rest of the academy, dark, damp, and cold. The lab is wildly bedraggled much like the professor. Jars of herbs, brews, and compounds scattered amongst an assortment of Dr. Spalding's research materials, line the stone walls. Old leather bound books, haphazardly disarrayed on the shelves that hold them, house many mysteries for each student to discover.

Professor Spalding, a short, disheveled, middle aged curmudgeon, often looses track of time and place when researching for his work. He sometimes will go for days without eating or bathing until some poor teary-eyed soul makes a comment on the effluvial effects he imprinted on the room. The Professor pulled his pocket watch out to check the time. "Where is that fool of a boy, and who are you people? How long have you Lilliputians been sneakin' around in my lab? Can't turn your back for two minutes without some strange folk and their shenanigans creeping up behind my back. Where is that boy, Fishbate?", the Professor grumbled. "It's Fishman Professor, and we are here for our lessons in Life Dimensions," Arron stated. "Jr. is late for everything, but he'll be here sooner or later, more than likely later," Melissa said. Melissa no sooner got the words out of her mouth when Jr. clambered through the door.

The Professor looked up from his microscope and gesticulated for his students to come see what he had prepared on the glass slide inserted in the microscope. "What is it you see when you look inside this scope children? Remember what the sample looks like, and keep it catalogued in your head so you can compare it to other samples," said the Professor. Each student took a turn gazing through the microscope and waited for further instructions. The Professor gave each student an eye dropper and instructed them to draw a sample of water out of the glass he had on his massive oak desk. He gave each student a specimen slide and had them put three drops per slide, being careful to maintain at least a two foot distance from each other while handling the specimens. They each had a turn looking at each other's specimens. "Can anyone explain to me what you have observed?" asked the professor. Melissa was the first to explain, "Well my water looks different from everyone else's water." "That's correct, and what else can you tell me?", the Professor beckoned as he looked intensely at each of them. "All three water samples of mine look the same but they look different from everyone else's," Arron said. "Exactly, and what does that tell us about water?", the Professor asked scowling at Jr. Jr. pondered the Professors question for a few minutes and thought about the data presented so far and said, "It seems that the water acts differently around each person, kinda showing each one of us something different." "Yes", the Professor expounded, "You see water has a memory, it takes on the properties of whatever it comes in contact with. The water now has a piece of you encoded in it. That is why the water appears different for each of you. Each one of you oscillates at a different rate, depending on what you are feeling and thinking at that moment. If you are angry and touch the water, it will appear ugly and disorganized under the microscope. If you have love, kindness, and peace in your thoughts while touching the water, it will appear like a beautiful crystal, pure clean, and balanced. You are effecting the life of the water with your personal vibrations, thoughts, and actions. So you see Jr., when you jumped in that mud puddle that is now a part of your khaki pants, you impressed aggression and lack of respect into the water. Is that what you want to contribute to the waters education? Who knows, the next disrespectful boy who comes across that puddle might end up imprinted with your aggression. Knowing a little bit about the personality of water gives new meaning to holy water or baptism, doesn't it?"

Professor Spalding went on to explain how special water is to all of us and how water communicates with itself and with all things. He told them how the amniotic fluid, that protects and nourishes an unborn baby in its mother's womb, has a similar composition to sea water. He explained how our bodies are comprised of mostly water. The Professor told his students to note, if water communicates with whatever it comes in contact with, and all things are comprised of mostly water, all things must communicate on a deeper level than we are aware. He explained how water is essential to every body function in all beings. The Professor said, "Water is the amniotic fluid of the universe and we must treat it with great respect." The Professor told his students to observe how water affects their lives. He asked the students to take special note of their thoughts while water is presenting itself to them in daily living. The students, freshly implanted with a powerful notion, finished up class for the day and made their way out the door.

"Wow, what a fabulous lesson we had today, can't wait to see what's next," Melissa exuberantly stated. "I'm gonna spend more time playing in the rain. Maybe take some of my stuff outside, that's if Momma lets me, and let it get acquainted with the wet stuff," Arron proclaimed. "How about you Jr., what do you think about the Professor's lesson today?", asked Melissa. "I feel a little funny about apologizing to a mud puddle. I have a feeling I'm gonna be doing a lot of apologizing this year," Jr. grumbled.

Arron's father, Adam Glassman, pulled his new Cadillac in front of the Wolff Academy for Gifted Children and honked the horn to get the children's attention. Melissa, Arron, and Jr. ran over to the car and said their hello's to Mr Glassman. "Awesome ride Mr Glassman. Can't wait till I have my own ride to impress the ladies," said Jr. "You kids want a lift?", asked Mr Glassman. A high pitched cacophony of yeas exploded into the air and the group all rushed to pile into the vehicle.

The Cadillac headed towards Melissa's house first. Just as Melissa scooted out of the car, a rain shower graced the afternoon with its presence. The delighted group rushed out of the car all at once to embrace the cool sprinkle. They ran around Melissa's yard giggling with their faces turned up and their arms outstretched till they ran out of breath and collapsed onto the wet grass. "See Jr, you did get something out of Professor Spalding's class or you wouldn't be out here in the rain with us acting crazy," said Melissa.

Melissa's mother, Janet, patiently waited for her daughter on the front porch. Muffled giggles surreptitiously climbed their way out of Janet's belly while she watched the children play in the rain. "Come on inside and get yourself ready for dinner Melissa, I think you have adequately drenched yourself for the day," beckoned Janet. "Ok Mom," Melissa replied as she worked her way to the cottage.

The Clark's cottage lies on the edge of the forest leaving the cacophonous intrusions of the city far behind. Bird gourds and multi colored cloth streamers hang from the trees outside the cottage. There is always a savory essence of Momma's home made bread floating in the air inducing a trance like state to an innocent passerby. A cozy country feel permeates the entire cottage with hand made doilies, heirlooms, antiques, and Janet's artwork. Janet Clark's art studio sits off to the side of the cottage filled with a multitude of fascinating sculptures and multimedia art. Melissa gets her passion for fashion from the inspirational environment her mother has created.

"How did school go for you today?", asked Janet. "It was fascinating Mom, we learned how water picks up information from us and remembers it. Professor Spalding says we should be mindful while we are touching the water and give it the respect it deserves. The professor is so funny with his pants falling down under his belly. He likes to pester Jr. by asking him questions when he is obviously not paying any attention, and that makes me laugh," replied Melissa. "You like Jr., don't you?", asked Janet. "I like to see him stumble around when he gets anywhere near me, and that makes me laugh too," said Melissa.

Jr. charged through the front door of the Fishman home announcing his presence. "I'm home Mom," Jr. shouted to the walls as his book bag fell to the floor. "When do we eat? I'm starving," hollered Jr. "Get your book bag off the floor and wash your hands for dinner," replied Mrs Fishman. Jr. complied to his mothers command and readied himself for dinner.

The Fishman's home exudes welcoming warmth to all that pass through its doors. Old Victorian charm married with town and country appeal gives each visitor a touch of days gone by. Bridgett Fishman will make anyone who steps into her home feel as if they are part of the family with her soft soothing voice and tender nature. Mrs. Fishman's breathtaking beauty and grace enchants any guest lucky enough to be in her presence. Clyde Fishman, Jr.'s father adds symmetry to the atmosphere with his powerful build and undaunted expressive nature.

Dinner at the Fishman's is nothing short of a signal event. It is no surprise to see the whole family in full King Arthur garb feasting like medieval royalty. Laughter is a priority.

"So Jr, how did your first day at the academy go?", asked Jr.'s father. "We learned that water is smart and can communicate with everything, it has a good memory too. We're supposed to pay more attention to what we are thinking and feeling and stuff while we are around any kind of water. I never gave water much thought before today's lesson, I thought it was just there to clean dishes and keep the fish floating. I don't think the professor likes me cuz he keeps givin me the stink eye," stated Jr. "you mean like this," Jr.'s father said as he bugged his eyes out and twisted his face up to resemble an ogre. "Now Clyde, stop playing around at the table, honestly you're worse than the kids," Mrs Fishman playfully scolded. Jr. and his two year old baby sister Katy laughed so hard they sprayed food all over themselves and each other. Clyde Fishman worked his way around the table to his wife Bridget, grabbed her by the waist and growled wildly while burrowing his face into her neck. "I'm going to have all of you for dinner," snarled Clyde Fishman. "Oh Clyde, go sit down and behave," said Bridgett.

CHAPTER 3

IT'S JUST A DREAM

MICKI EVRIS

*T*HE DAY SURRENDERED TO the night fall as Melissa and Arron went to sleep dreaming of rain showers and dew drop sprites whispering mystical secrets in their ears. Have the misty midnight guides come to tutor them into higher states of consciousness? What will they learn as they sleep? Will they heed any lessons gifted to them?

Jr. fell into an unusually deep sleep on this misty night. Within minutes of closing his eyes, a sparkling diamond vortex enveloped his body. Millions of images, to fast to be distinguishable, flashed in Jr.'s mind. He felt like a black hole, sucking in pieces of the universe around him. When he finally hit full capacity a vibrant stream of gold light burst out the top of Jr.'s head, illuminating his surroundings. He found himself on a pacific island, walking down a narrow dirt path leading to an estuary surrounded by coconut palm trees. Something shimmering softly just ahead of him caught his attention and Jr. couldn't resist getting a closer look.

A beautiful young woman, birthed from the estuary she was fashioned by, stood by one of the palm trees singing a wistful song. Her long wavy hair trailed down the length of her body to her slender waist modestly covering her gracefully alluring figure. A luminous shimmer permeated her being, leaving many a young boy enchanted by her delicate elegance. Jr. cautiously approached the doleful water woman and asked, "Excuse me madam, are you alright, why are you singing such a sad song?" The woman turned to look at Jr. and replied, "I have been taken for granted by all the people of this earth. No one appreciates the life I carry within my drops or the refreshment I supply to the parched earth. I have baptized the souls of many with my graces and received a smattering of gratitude. I safely house and nourish the embryo of each creature on this planet. I carry the thoughts of creation within me and safely offer them to all, great and small. When will I be seen?" As the wistful woman once again commenced a mournful wailing, a stormy sky began to pour forth a deluge swallowing up the land.

Jr. awakened in a panic gasping for air, thinking he was under water. "I've gotta stop her from crying us into extinction. I have to tell her.... Where am I, am I dreaming? Oh man, I gotta get ready for class!", Jr. gasped as he shot out of bed running late again.

Once again, the three friends found their way to Professor Spalding's class much the same way as they did before with Melissa arriving first, followed by Arron, and Jr. crashing through the door in a huff at the last minute. "Why is it you children have to make so much noise with everything you do? Who is making that entire ruckus? Oh you again, Fishbate," Professor Spalding snarled. "It's Fishman," said Jr. "Yes, yes, I have the unfortunate awareness of knowing exactly who you are Fishbate. Your mother was one of my top student's back in the day. I can only hope you have half the brains and talent your mother had when she was in this same class."

The Professor was, as usual, fidgeting with a half dozen projects at the same time, with each project layered on top of the other, making complete chaos of the lab. Paper stickies hanging off his shirt and forehead reminding him of something that needs to be done in the near future. "What in tarnation did I do with my notes for today's class? I swear someone comes in here and moves things around just to get my dander up. Fishbate, get over here and help me find the notes for today's class." Jr. jumped to the professor's command and immediately found what the professor had misplaced. Jr. reached up and hesitantly pealed the sticky note off the professor's forehead. "I think this is what you are looking for Professor," Jr. said with a self-satisfied look on his face. "Smart aleck," the professor grumbled as he snatched the note from Jr.'s hand. "Now go sit down with the rest of the Lilliputians. Jr. found the seat saved for him by his best buds Arron and Melissa and plopped down into it.

"Now, does anyone want to report any illuminations received about the water assignment you worked on yesterday?", asked the professor as he scowled at the students. John Parker raised his hand for recognition. John is very anemic in appearance, with his skin being almost transparent. His slithering, reptilian mannerisms creates an eerie, enigmatic persona; isolating him from his peers. The professor gesticulated for John to speak. "I had nightmares last night about being swallowed up by an angry and powerful sea, but two humongous lizard-like creatures got me out of there if I promised to help them later. I would have promised them my little sister to get out of there, she gets on my nerves anyway. These guys where as big as a dinosaur, had enough teeth to eat T-Rex, and swallowed up the daylight when they opened their mouths. They called themselves Plio and Mosas. I couldn't tell if I peed my pants or was drenched by the sea when I woke up."

The Professor's face sallowed and his knees buckled under him. "Did you say Plio and Mosas?", the Professor asked. "Uh huh, I'm glad it was just a stupid dream," replied John. "What did you promise them John?" John, now starting to look as panic stricken as the Professor, asked, "why, did I do something wrong? Oh crap, I'm in trouble ain't I?" "Let's just say it's not just a stupid dream John," said the Professor.

"You children need to know, that from now on, don't take anything for granted and think before you open up that cavity infested fly traps you call your mouths," the Professor scolded. The children all sat a little straighter in their seats and their grins turned into worry wrinkles in a real hurry. "The Professor is not playing around," said Melissa. Her fellow classmates all nodded in agreement. "The Professor is freaking out about something," Arron noted. The Professor grumbled under his breath for a good five minutes while horbgorbling about the room, then told the students to take a break.

After a good while, the students slowly eased back into the lab to avoid any retribution from the professor. The Professor was desperately rifling through one of the large leather bound books he acquired from the lab's library, shouting out a single word here and there, and scribbling bits and pieces of information on scraps of paper. The class sensed a great urgency in the professor's flailing. They skillfully tip-toed past the Professor and made their way back to their seats.

The Professor took a deep breath trying to control his impatience, unsuccessfully I might add, and addressed the class. "There is this round object that resides somewhere between your shoulders that's suppose to contain something known as THE BRAIN. Now this BRAIN, unbeknownst to most of you, is there to obtain and retain useful information to assist you throughout the rest of your miserable Lilliputian lives, in becoming useful, productive adults. I can only hope that, by the time you graduate, you can find this BRAIN, and put it to good use! Now let's get on with the lesson, shall we?

"Now John, you say you met these two sea monsters called Plio and Mosas? Can you remember what you promised to do for them?", the professor asked. John replied, "Yes sir, they asked me to call for them by name whenever I get angry or fearful. They told me that nothing pleases them more than absorbing hatred, anger, and fear. I agreed to do what they asked me to do, it's just a dream, what's the big deal?" The professor, still trying to contain his impatience, is now turning red in the face and delivering low pitched grumblings into the atmosphere. "What if I told you that it's not just a dream? Would you continue on with this promise and feed these vile creatures the putrid, rotting byproduct of hatred, anger, and fear?" John Parker, beginning to grow tired of the professor's scolding, retorted, "Look, I don't believe in the reality of this dream, in fact, it all sounds pretty stupid. It's just a bad dream, nothing else. You need to retire old man."

The students held their breath waiting for the professor's reaction to their classmate's insubordination. The Professor took a deep breath, calmed himself, and plopped himself in the seat behind his desk. Realizing he had his work cut out for him, the Professor stopped to rethink his teaching strategies to accommodate this new batch of Lilliputians. "Let's start fresh tomorrow, class dismissed for the day."

The children piled out of Professor Spalding's class, grateful to be relieved from the days pressured experience. "What was that all about? The professor was super upset about something," queried Melissa. "I don't know, hopefully we'll find out tomorrow," said Arron.

Jr. had a puzzled look on his face and seemed detached from the conversation. "You're awful quiet, what's wrong Jr.?", asked Melissa. Jr. revealed his dream experience, "I didn't get a chance to tell the Professor about the strange dream I had. John's dream had some of the same stuff in it my dream had, except mine had a bodaciously gorgeous lady in it instead of two ugly sea monsters. A spiral of water from the ocean inlet rose up into the air and formed a beautiful woman. She was upset about not being appreciated. Her dedication to the service of all beings, great and small, has been ignored and now she's really pissed. She cried so hard, she totally wiped out the land. I tried to stop her, but I woke up before I could do anything about it. I have a feeling there's a big storm ahead of us one way or another. I'm almost afraid to go to sleep tonight. I hope nothing weird happens when I start dreaming." Jr. stated. "I'm praying I won't remember a thing about my dreams, not after hearing about yours and John's," said Arron.

Jr. quickened his step and waved good by to his friends. "See you guys later. I'm gonna head on home, I'm starved," said Jr. "You're always starved," teased Melissa. Arron nodded in agreement. Jr. quickly became a small speck in the dust ahead of Melissa and Arron as he sprinted down the road towards home. Arron and Melissa followed suit, safely making their own way home, anticipating a wild and crazy, yet insightful night of lucid dreaming.

CHAPTER 4

WHAT ARE YOU DOING HERE?

THE SEEDING

*J*R. FOUND HIMSELF WALKING down the same pacific island pathway that brought him to the mysterious estuary woman he encountered the night before. The sound of footsteps heading straight for him made his heart pound hard enough to be heard outside of his body. Suddenly Jr. realized he was not alone on the island. In fact, the sound of scurried movement from several different directions became apparent. Jr. took cover behind a large coconut tree and waited to see who or what was coming. He grabbed a large stick he found on the ground next to his foot and hung on tight in preparation for an altercation. Two rapidly moving figures from opposite directions collided and fell to the ground in a heap. Jr. carefully poked his head from around the tree to get a better look at what was going on. "What are you two doing here?", gasped Jr. Arron and Melissa, rubbing their aching body parts, looked up to see their friend Jr standing in front of them. "What are you doing here?", chimed Arron and Melissa. Jr. helped his two stunned friends to their feet and all three hugged each other with great relief.

"Where are we?", asked Melissa. "You're on the island in my dream I told you guys about," explained Jr. "How can that be happening? How can all of us be in the same dream?", asked Arron. "I haven't the slightest idea. I'm just happy it's you guys and not some bug eyed alien from Mars," Jr. replied. "What's the plan now?", asked Arron. "I'll take you guys to the spot I saw the hot tamale made out of water," Jr. said.

As Jr., Arron, and Melissa approached the estuary, they heard grotesque guttural mutterings and, what seemed to be, a human voice talking. The companions slowed their steps, cautiously approaching the estuary, stopping short of arrival to gain insight of the bizarre conversation they heard. "That voice sounds familiar," Melissa whispered. Arron and Jr. nodded in agreement. They stealthily craned their necks around the tree that shields them to catch a glimpse of the precarious situation. "Holy moly! That's John and those two sea monsters Plio and Mosas!", Jr. gasped. "Shhhh, let's not let them know we're here. We'll be goners for sure," Melissa shuddered as she spoke. The children silenced themselves in fear and trepidation, listening to the malevolent powwow between John and the two evil sea monsters. "Where is the hot tamale you told us about?", whispered Arron. Jr. peered out as far as he dared to see if he could find the beautiful woman. Melissa tapped Jr. on the shoulder and pointed towards a large boulder at the edge of the water. There, precariously draped over the giant rock, was Jr.'s water woman. "She looks like she's dying," said Melissa. The once vibrantly beautiful marine maiden, was lying lifeless, in a brackish stench, enveloped by the slime of leaches. "They did something to her. Those scum balls are gonna pay for this!", Jr. cried, as he leaped forward to attack. Melissa and Arron restrained him as they covered his mouth to prevent detection and total annihilation.

Plio's nostrils pulsed wildly with each breath as he craned his neck higher to feed his senses further. "The putrid scent of innocence violates the air I breath. Who's there?", Plio thundered. Hysterical screams echoed through the atmosphere as the three companions scrambled to grip the ground with their whirling feet.

Beep, beep, beep… The sounding alarm made Jr. jumps a foot off the bed as he continued to scream, as if he was still dreaming. "Are you alright up there?", hollered his mother. Jr. shook his head in confusion trying to figure out what just happened. "It's time for school. Get those lazy bones moving young man," Mrs. Fishman commanded. "Ok Mom, I'll be there in a jiffy," replied Jr., as he reoriented himself for the new day ahead of him.

Jr., Arron, and Melissa rendezvoused outside of the academy to discuss what to do about their encounter with John, Plio, and Mosas. They all agreed to get the professor involved, but they wanted to do it on the down low. "I think we should ask the Professor what to do after class, that way we can keep it on a need to know basis and not freak everyone out. We need to keep John out of the loop as well," Jr. stated. Arron and Melissa agreed.

Professor Spalding's Lilliputians' assembled reluctantly into the lab anticipating a cantankerous interlude of retributions from the professor. The class painstakingly waited for the lesson du jour. The Professor, engrossed in his studies, finally looked up to address the class. "That was the most orderly assemblage I have ever seen, and Fishbate, you're here on time, without a ruckus to boot! By George, it's a dad-blamed miracle, you've all located your brains!" The Professor smiled with delight.

The Professor stood up from his desk and announced to the class, "We are going to do something a little different today. We're going to the academy garden. Go to the lockers, on the south wall of the classroom, and pick up a blanket and pillow to take to the garden." The children did as instructed and grabbed what they needed for the excursion. John went out of his way to bogart the space Jr. was occupying and rudely snatched the pillow out of Jr.'s hands. "That pillow has my name on it," John snarled. "Hey! what did you do that for? This isn't a Macy's sale ya know," Jr. retorted.

The Professor purposefully cleared his throat and gave the two boys a raised eye brow, the stink eye, as Jr would call it. John gave Jr one last shove and went on his way. "What was that about?", asked Melissa. "I haven't a clue. The guy has major attitude issues," said Jr. "Come on guys, let's get to the garden," added Arron. The students gathered all the needed supplies and headed for the academy garden.

The academy garden is a classic English storybook vision, with three acres of roses and herbs, two serpentine lakes, yellow laburnum walkways, and a hornbeam hedge maze. The labyrinth is a mammoth temptation for any twelve year old child to try to stay clear of.

The Professor directed the class to find a comfortable spot by the rhododendron garden waterfall and spread their blankets out on the ground. "Lie down and get comfortable, we are all going on a magic carpet ride," instructed Professor Spalding. The students, delighted to be outside and out of the classroom, did as they where told with great exuberance.

"This is great, a good nap is just what we need to balance the brain," said Arron. As Arron realized what he just said, he abruptly turned, looking wide eyed at Jr. and Melissa, and swallowed hard in anticipation of another dream event. "What if we fall asleep? Should we devise a plan to keep each other awake?" Arron frantically queried. Jr. replied, "The Professor will notice if we're not participating in the assignment. God knows, we don't want to upset the professor. Let's just hope this magic carpet takes an alternate route."

Professor Spalding lulled the students into a deep relaxed state in preparation for a dream journey. His voice, out of character for the crotchety Professor, was soft and soothing and had a smooth steady rhythm. He had the students fill their being with the atmosphere of the garden habitat. "Let the particles you are made of commingle with the beauty of the garden. Do not anticipate or expect anything, just be as the garden is." The Professor's voice echoed into nothingness as the children took their magic garden carpet ride.

CHAPTER 5

THE SEEDING

MICKI EVRIS

*J*R., ARRON, AND MELISSA slowly became conscious of each other's presence. They found themselves in the middle of the garden labyrinth. Jr. took charge, "Ok guys, let's not panic. We have each other, and we have some experience with the dream world already. Let's stick together and see where this maze takes us."

The scent of roses and honeysuckle filled the air as beautiful blue butterflies delightfully danced about. A striking red fox offered companionship along the way and birds gleefully chattered while gathering breakfast. "Wow, this is truly paradise. I could stay here forever," Melissa swooned. The children marveled at the beauty charitably unfolding in front of them. As they walked further, a storm cloud formed ahead of them. "I knew it was all going too well, there had to be a thorn in the bush somewhere," Arron stated. Little by little, the butterflies disappeared, the perfumed air turned putrid, and the fox cowered fearfully behind them. A stagnant pool of brackish water blocked their passage. Maggots overtook the decomposing foliage on the path beneath their feet. The air was heavy with a foggy gloom. Jr. held his arm out to prevent his companions from going any further. "Look who's here," Jr. gesticulated for his friends to look ahead. "No wonder everything turned to crap, John the Jerk is here," Arron said.

John was standing at the edge of the stagnant pool of stench. He had gathered a fair amount of butterflies together and put them in a jar. One by one he took them out, crumbled them to dust in his fist and fed them to the decay. John began to chant in a low pitched guttural voice, "I offer to you all my hate, fear, and unkind thoughts. I have taken the life and beauty from these garden beings and turned them to dust for your pleasure. I am forever your servant. I feed to you the energy of innocence to use as you will."

A foul steam rose from the stagnant pool out of which a creature from the underworld had formed. It resembled a prehistoric reptile with four flippers, like it's father, had a giant mouth built for destruction. "I am X, son of Plio. You have pleased me with your offerings of destruction and pain. You are a loyal servant and shall be rewarded for your deeds. My father has a message for you John. Come closer, I will deliver his unhallowed bidding. You have been seeded with my fathers malevolence. He names you the Prince of Despair. You shall inseminate depravity and wickedness into the mental fluids of mankind. We are at war, and you are my father's soldier, the commander of death and decay. My father's seed will grow and fester in the ignorant mist of the human mind, as it did in yours."

Jr. and his two companions, aghast and filled with trepidation, quietly retreated to safer ground. "We need to get back to the professor before John and that evil thing realize we know what they are up to," Jr. vehemently stated. "What's the plan?", queried Arron. "We will ourselves back to the awake state, meet up in the garden, and get some help from the Professor," explained Jr.

The three allies expeditiously grabbed the first magic carpet ride out of Dodge and hightailed it back to the Professor. Jr. awakened in a flash, landing on his blanket in the garden. Professor Spalding hovered over Jr. with trepidation overtaking his expression. "What's going on Fishbate? I got one of those gut feelings you and your cohorts got yourselves into some kind of trouble. Been waiting for you to snap back to this plane of reality. Time to spill the beans, boy."

Melissa and Arron, now fully awake, wasted no time finding their way to the professor. The three students proceeded to slog the professor with a flurried cacophony of squawks and shrills while tumultuously describing the days dream event. "I always figured John for a lowlife, but this is over the top," Arron stated. The befuddled professor implored the children to slow down and explain in a comprehensible manner, "what's this blubbering about John feeding demons dusty butterflies and inseminating the servants?" All three children let out a synchronous moan as they tried to gather composure.

Jr. took a deep breath, gathering courage to explain, once again, the disquieting dream experience to the Professor. A flurry of words spilled out of Jr.'s mouth, "We all saw John in the dream world making a pact with X, Plio's son. You know Plio, the sea monster John told us about in class?" The professor gestured with an affirmative nod that he understood. Jr. continued, "John is feeding fear, hate, and the essence of innocence to Plio and his son, X. There is supposed to be some kind of dark shadow war and John is the appointed command - ant, or commander, or something like that. They're gonna plant seeds in our minds to turn us into evil low life zombies, like they did to John. Is that possible? How can we fix this? We need to put the pedal to the metal Professor." Melissa and Arron briskly nodded their heads in agreement.

The Professor started pacing, throwing his hands up in the air as he talked to the sky, "What in tarnation have you got me into now. These tormenting Lilliputians haven't a clue what they've gotten themselves into. Must I embark on this mission of war girded with an army of ants?" The professor paced back and forth for a good while, grumbling and pulling at his hair. In an instant, the professor stopped dead in his tracks and appeared to be listening to something. "Must I remind you, many giants have fallen by the hand of the bitty," said the small voice within the professor, scolding him into submission. "OK, OK, I give. I can see you're not going to let me out of this, so let's get on with it," the Professor grumbled as he looked to the sky.

The Professor, yielding to the higher good, gathered the three Lilliputians into a huddle to thrash out a battle plan. The disquieted Professor, now looking quite disheveled from pulling at his hair, making it stand on end, made it difficult for the three students to look at him with any seriousness. "What in tarnation are you three looking at? Do I have something growing out of the side of my neck?", the Professor snarled. Melissa, Jr., and Arron pointed at the Professor's hair and tried desperately to hold back their amusement, to no avail. "It appears that I'm stuck with the lot of you. You're all unfledged hatchlings still wet behind the ears. By the time we're finished with this mission you'll be grey, surly, and talking to yourselves just like me," the Professor snarled. The children gasped at the thought of becoming anything like the gnarly old Professor. "Let's focus, shall we?", the Professor commanded. "Jr., we have got to get your mother in on this, her resplendent spirit will help replenish the luminosity snuffed out by Plio and Mosas. Tell your mother the battle has begun and we're gathering up the troops. Let's rendezvous at Jr.'s house tonight after dinner. I'll call your parents' and tell them we have a group assignment." The children all agreed with the plan. The Professor, Jr., Arron, and Melissa walked back to the lab together in silence, anticipating the frightful battle ahead of them.

By this time, the rest of the students had returned from dream time and headed back to the classroom. As John sauntered his way back to the lab, he perused the faces of his unsuspecting classmates while plotting the demise of their innocence. The taste of power amplified John's craving, making him desire more and more of its addictive flavor. The sacrifice and betrayal of friendship is a small price to pay for eternal power in John's wilted mind.

The Professor purposely cleared his throat to alert the students it was time to pay attention. "Why does everything you children do have to involve constant jabbering? Fold up your blankets and put them back in an orderly fashion. We are finished for the day. I want a detailed report describing the experience you had today while in dream time. What did you feel, taste, smell, and hear while you were dreaming? Were you able to change or affect the outcome of your experience? You have the entire weekend to put something on paper, that doesn't involve the use of crayons. Show me you can use your brain. No excuses for late assignments. No peanut butter and jelly paragraph embellishments. Class dismissed."

CHAPTER 6

THE WHOLE STORY

As PLANNED, THE RENDEZVOUS started promptly after dinner at the Fishman home. The dinner table cleared of food, and now holding leather bound portfolios, maps, books, and notes from the professor's personal stash and Mrs. Fishman's undisclosed collection. The professor and Mrs Fishman arranged to have Arron and Melissa spend the weekend at the Fishman home, under the guise of a group outing.

"Ok kids, it's time to let us know everything, and I mean everything about what you have been up to," the Professor commanded. Jr. told the Professor and his mother about the two encounters with the water woman, John's alliance with the sea monsters, and revisited the garden dream experience. Arron and Melissa recapitulated their experience as well. Bridgett Fishman and the Professor, agog with the telling of the tale, gazed at each other in a catatonic stupor. The Professor broke the silence and asked Bridgett, "Are you thinking what I'm thinking?" "Marilla!", the Professor and Bridget simultaneously shouted. The three children jolted a foot above their seats from the shout. "Who's Marilla?", Melissa asked.

The Professor took a long deep breath, reached deep into his archival memories, and began reminiscing. "Back in the day, when Jr.'s mother was my most prized apprentice, we went exploring in dream time. Just like the three of you, Bridgett and I collided on that same island, nearly knocking each other's heads off. Scared the tarnation out of both of us. Neither of us realized we could be in each other's dream space. We quickly adapted to each other's space and explored the island together. We heard this compelling, enchanting, most liquidizing sound coming from the estuary. We had no choice but to investigate. There she was, Marilla, breathtakingly beautiful, delightfully fused with the motion of the waterfall, serenading the dawn of its existence. She gave birth to the fall she was made of. I was captivated by her splendor, probably more so than Bridgett, as most men or young boys would naturally be." Jr., Arron, and the professor paused for a moment and sighed, overcome with the gleaming image of Marilla, indelibly etched in their virile minds. Bridgett cleared her throat loud enough to break the spell as Melissa gave Jr. a playful slap on the shoulder. The boys snapped out of their mesmeric state looking a bit sheepish and momentarily befuddled. "Why don't you take over from here Bridgett? Tell them the rest of the story," the Professor implored.

Bridgett paused to bring her recollection to the forefront of her mind. "As the professor was saying, before he got sidetracked...we were witnessing one of the purest forms of love ever seen on this earth. Marilla loved the sea so much, she gave herself to it and it gave itself to her in return. It was creation itself manifesting right there in front of us. Their offspring is the perpetuation of aquatic fluidity. The sky cradles their children in a bed of clouds." Melissa swooned, "oh how romantic. I'll never see clouds the same way again."

Bridgett continued," the Professor and I approached Marilla, hoping to engage her in dialogue.

She beckoned us to come closer. She delighted us with a gentle mist, inviting us to partake of her fluid-being in order to understand her. She had us close our eyes and open our minds. She told us to breathe in and feel the rhythm of the waterfall. As we exhaled, we let our bodies dissipate into the pulsating fluid to become one being. At that moment, we realized everything is one fluid energy being. We not only merged with Marilla and the waterfall, we merged with all things. Pure love permeated every particle of existence. Our perception of all that is, magnified and matured. Compassion for the inconsequential became strikingly momentous. Everything was significant, just as it is now and always will be. We were transformed forever. No longer would we take things for granted or see anything as less than we are."

"Wow! what an amazing experience. Do you think we can come to understand things the way you and the professor do?", asked Melissa. Bridgett replied to Melissa's query, "If you so desire to. The main ingredient to obtain anything you have a hunger for, whether it be for gaining knowledge or obtaining a skill, is to maintain a fervent passion for it. You must feel the thing you desire has always been a part of your being, and you just became aware of its presence in you. Be grateful for the gift you have already been given. When you do this, you will activate the energetic lattice that surrounds you and everything will work together to bring about your desire."

Bridgett continued, "Listen carefully, all of you, for the things the Professor and I are telling you will arm you for the fight ahead of us. You are Initiates of the Primordial Light. You have been chosen, along with the Professor and I, to ensure germination occurs in the Seeds of Light that lie dormant in the minds of man. Marilla brings fluid dynamic activity to these inert embryonic mind seeds. Without the liquid matrix Marilla supplies, the seeds remain unfurled, lifeless, and without lineage. Marilla is dying as we speak. John, Plio, and Mosas are working to destroy Marilla and Earth's matrix, creating an infertile environment in the minds of unconscious beings. Eventually we will become primitive beings, Earth will loose its connection with the Universal Matrix, and energetic restructuring will inevitably occur."

CHAPTER 7

TRAINING THE LILLIPUTIANS

"*When do we start* training for the mission?", asked Arron. The Professor answered, "you already have a pretty good start with your abilities in maneuvering your consciousness in dream time. Bridgett and I will help you refine your technique. Tonight you will learn how to dematerialize your dense form and blend your energy with a higher light form. We all need to gather pure energy, fuse with Marilla, and bring her back into balance."

"Does anyone need a potty break before we get started? Speak now or forever hold your pee. Once we get started, there will be no time to stop for a bladder that dilly-dallies", the professor grumbled and said a few choice words under his breath about immature, Lilliputian urine sacs. Everyone rushed to get up from the table to take care of business. While waiting her turn to gain entrance to the powder room, Melissa expressed her excitement about the mission to Arron, "I can't believe we are about to embark on the most important mission of our lives. Our worlds existence depends on us…us…,the miserable Lilliputians from Nowheresville. Isn't it awesome?" Arron, looking pensive, answered, "What if we lose the battle? This is a huge responsibility. We need to focus like we never have before. Like you said, our whole worlds existence depends on US! My urine sac can't contain itself thinking about it."

With the children out of earshot, Bridgett approached the professor with concern, "I'm worried this is too much for the children to handle. Do you think they're up for it?" The Professor responded, "I never would have guessed this group of microscopic larvae would be the chosen initiates the world would have to depend on for its survival. I have to say, despite their tiny pint sized brains, they work well together and adapt quickly to new and unusual circumstances. I'm gonna have to wash my mouth out with soap for saying this but, I think they'll be just fine. If you tell anyone I said that, I'll deny ever knowing you and mark you off my Christmas list for life." Bridgett chuckled and gave the professor a playful push on the shoulder, which he thoroughly enjoyed. "We better get back to the children before they get themselves into trouble," said Bridgett.

The group gathered back at the table after their break. Bridgett told the children to get comfortable in their chairs and prepare for a guided meditation. "We are going to fuse our personal energy particles with pure love. We need to gather as much pure love energy as possible to recharge the Matrix. With all of us pinpointing our focus on one specific task, the results will be amplified one hundred fold. We will do a few practice runs to hone our skills, then coalesce our energies. Close your eyes and feel the space around you. Take long deep breaths and melt into the space you occupy. Feel the space around you enter your body as you inhale. The space is soothing and relaxes your body as you breathe it in. Now think of something you love more than anything. Find the spot in your body this love originates from and let it expand outward with each exhalation. This love is gentle and smooth, has no boundaries or limitations, it is not demanding or conditional, it is perfect. The space around you is filled with this same impeccable love. You inhale the love from the space around you and exhale love back into this space. Keep inhaling and exhaling till there is no difference in the space around you and the space within you. You feel yourself dissipate into pure love, you are love, and all is as it should be. There is only one space, where all things exist, and you are all things. Reside here and just be in the experience." The children felt the borders of their bodies evanesce, amalgamating their true essence with the space around them. Bridgett gave the children ample time to absorb the experience then gently called them back, "Slowly bring your awareness back to your body, the room, and the chair you are sitting in. Open your eyes."

The children looked around the table at each other, smiling in recognition of the oneness they all shared, maintaining a gentle euphoric silence. Bridgett broke the spell and asked, "Well, any thoughts?" Melissa responded, "there is nothing that will ever top that experience. I am complete. Thank you so much for that." Arron expressed his gratitude with a few joyful tears and hugged everyone in the room. Jr. couldn't stop saying, "Wow!, Wow!,and, Wow!" Bridgett and the Professor mentored the three compadres through a few more meditations before moving on to the next lesson.

The Professor suggested everyone take a short break to let the lesson settle into all the right spaces. "Let's go outside on the front porch for some fresh air, stretch our legs, and clear our mental palate." "Is this some kind of marathon initiate training? How much do we have to learn this weekend? I'm itching to get my hands on John and those slimy bottom feeders Plio, Mosas, and X," Jr. vehemently stated. The Professor answered, "I never intended to get this deep into training in such a short time, but to my enormous surprise, the three of you have been chosen for this mission by the Devine Cosmos, and the Devine Cosmos says now is the time. Many lifetimes of experienced training will have to be digested in a millisegment of your life, but for the moment, let's just relax and breathe in some fresh air before we start thinking about what's next on the agenda." So the motley crew of cosmic crusaders, seasoned and neophyte, indulged their senses with the caress of the evening breeze. "Is everyone ready to go back inside the house and commence training?", asked Bridgett. Without a word, the group herded back into the house and took their seats at the table.

THE SEEDING

The Professor addressed the children. "The next task will be learning to identify your thoughts and where they originate from. That should be easy enough to do, since you don't use your brain to hold any thoughts to begin with." "Professor,…..be nice!", Bridgett gently scolded. "Oh you're no fun at all," the professor grumbled. The Professor continued, "we are going to sit in silence." The Professor abruptly paused to shoot an accusing scowl at Jr., daring him to make the slightest sound. "We will sit and do nothing, in silence, till you get bored enough to start talking to yourselves. This mental chatter is what programs the subconscious mind and the matrix to create future circumstances, circumstances you might not have willingly wished upon yourself or anyone else."

The group sat in dead silence for a good half hour. The mental chatter started to intrude into their susceptible minds, as the Professor foretold. Melissa's chatter started with wondering what she was going to wear tomorrow, which led to wondering what Jr. would like to see her wear, which lead to Jr. and herself on a romantic getaway island, which turned into the dream island and the water woman, which finally segwayed into John's a creepy no-account jerk for messing with Marilla and everyone's minds. Jr.'s mind talk started with wondering if they were going to get something to eat soon, which lead to sitting at the dinner table with the group, which lead to reviewing the dream world conversation, which segwayed into John's a creepy no-account jerk for messing with Marilla and everyone's heads. Arron started wondering what the most efficient battle strategy would be, which lead to worrying about the outcome of the battle, which finally transitioned to John's a creepy no-account jerk for messing with Marilla and everyone's minds.

The Professor cleared his throat loud enough to bring everyone into the awareness of the now. "Jr, let's start with the thoughts that seeped into your mind, that's if you have any thoughts at all." Jr. exposed his inner jabbering to the group, which reminded him once again how hungry he is. "When are we going to break for a snack?", Jr. asked. Melissa rolled her eyes and chimed, "Oh my God, is that all you think about?" Jr. shrugged his shoulders up to his ears and gave a sheepish, "I can't help it" look. "Why am I not surprised", the professor grumbled as he turned to ask Arron and Melissa to recount their musings. As the three initiates realized they all segwayed into the same end thought, they indulged themselves with a good dose of cathartic laughter to lighten up the heavy atmosphere. The Professor let a deep-gut chuckle escape from his inner child and admitted, thinking about John did not generate the most positive feelings in himself either.

Bridgett, happy to see the Professor relate to the children for once, continued to educate the initiates. "Do you see how quickly your mind tries to fill the silent spaces with anything it can grab a-hold of. Sometimes that long chain of chatter can lead you off the beaten path to a dark and doleful space. Some people never find their way back. Most of the time we are unaware of this continuous babbling and the hypnotic affect it has on us. We often review unpleasant or hurtful past circumstances, holding onto them for years, as if we couldn't live without them. We pummel our hearts with the pain of the past, afraid to let go of it. We doom our future to be beholden to our request for more of the same. I will give you an example: You go for a walk. You notice a ditch in the road. The ditch looks just like the hole you threw yourself into to avoid getting shot at when you were in the war. You think of your best friend dying next to you in that ditch. You are now depressed for the rest of your walk and see everything from that depressing perspective. You let you're thoughts dictate how you feel and respond to future events by not taking control of them in the now. Another example: You do something stupid. Your mother yells at you and tells you you'll never learn. You not only feel like an idiot, you have lost your mothers respect. You feel rejected and insecure.

THE SEEDING

You start telling yourself you can't do anything right and are too dense to learn anything. Ten years later, you have repeated these same words to yourself over and over again without realizing it. You now can't retain any teaching and have flunked out of school. You have programmed yourself for failure. You generate an ambiance around yourself that reeks rejection. The matrix sympathetically complies with your design and brings your request for failure into fruition.

Bridgett explained, "It's imperative, for your evolution, that you remain vigilant in identifying the idle chatter filling the fertile spaces in your minds. Stop the chatter in it's tracks and purposefully plant useful thoughts to bring about positive growth. For example: You are worried about a test you have to take at school. You start doubting your ability to reason through the test questions. Instead of continuing this train of thought till you no longer have any self esteem, take charge of the next thought. Remind yourself of the positive results you had in the past. Spend your time preparing further for the test. Relax and absorb feelings of confidence and trust as you study. The more you relax with it, the more open you are to obtaining and retaining information."

Arron asked, "How can we be on guard constantly of the thoughts that creep into our minds and stay relaxed at the same time?" Bridgett explained, "When you identify and reject feelings of fear and doubt then replace it with feelings of peace and love, your body will no longer provide resistance to the energy pathways that reside throughout your entire being. While you are in a peaceful state, even in the midst of chaos, your mind and body will open its energy pathways to receive valuable information about what you need to know or do next. While you are in a fearful state, your body tightens up and blocks the energy pathways that carry important information." Arron asked, "So we pretend fear is not there?" Bridgett replied, "No, you acknowledge the fear is there, be grateful that it made itself obvious enough for you to clear, then choose not to identify yourself with it. Breathe yourself into a peaceful state and identify with that instead. If you do not feel peace, remember a circumstance when you did, and summon that feeling into the now. Practice summoning up feelings of peace, love, and joy as often as possible, feel it vibrate through your entire body. These higher vibrational feelings will protect you and help you relax and respond with impeccability in times of adversity, or at anytime for that matter. You will be able to feel if something is "off" in the space around you by maintaining higher vibrational feelings."

To clarify the lesson on clearing your thoughts, Bridgett gave a summation, "Relax your body. Breathe in peace and love FROM the space around you. Exhale peace and love INTO the space around you. Be a passive observer to the thoughts that enter your mind. Let your thoughts come and go without resistance or ownership. Let your subconscious clean itself out. Make no judgements. This should be your daily routine. After practicing this routine for a while, the idle chatter cannot burrow into your subconscious mind. The chatter will be an obvious contrast against the placid state of being you have fostered. You will also notice when outside thoughts pop into your mind, thoughts from someone or something else, you may choose to communicate with them at this time or let those thoughts pass by as well. You will also be privy to inter-dimensional communication with higher beings. This is Dr. Spalding's area of expertise. Professor, would you like to continue from here?" "Yes, I think I can take it from here. Your teachings are superlative, as usual, my dear. Before we continue, let's take another break for a snack before that son of yours starts eating the furniture."

The five cosmic crusaders took a much needed break to empty their urine sacs, shut Jr up with some food, and indulge in some lighter conversation. Jr. asked, "What does all this stuff we're learning have to do with kicking the arrogance clean out of John's power hungry ego? Marilla is dying as we speak." The Professor answered, "Be patient my boy, you only have to learn a couple more things before we head out on our journey. I promise, you will understand what it's all about shortly. It all sounds very exciting now but you might have different thoughts when you're standing face to face in front of Plio, Mosas, and X. You must maintain complete control of your emotions at all times to win this battle. Hatred, anger, and fear will only add strength to our adversaries." Jr. quickly switched his focus, as he took a big bite out of the sandwich his mother placed in front of him. "This is great Mom. I was starving. Thanks." The group chuckled unanimously, as they watched Jr. devour his sandwich in the blink of an eye. Bridgett's homemade bread, fixins, and left over pot roast hit the spot for everyone at the table. No one uttered a word for a good fifteen minutes. The professor broke the silence, "Well my dear, you sure know how to make a surly old man purr like a baby kitten. This is absolutely marvelous. When this is all over, I'm gonna steal you away from that husband of yours." Bridgett replied, "Clyde might have a thing or two to say about that, but you're welcome for dinner anytime." Everyone stuffed themselves to their fullest capacity and proceeded to help clear the table.

"Professor, could you give us an idea how we will be using the techniques you are teaching tonight for this battle ahead of us?", Arron queried. The professor took a moment to gather his thoughts, and then answered, "The meditations will help you join with Marilla and the Divine. Clearing your thoughts will prevent negative influences and enable you to receive instruction from the Divine. We will become a conduit for Divine energy to heal Marilla and nullify any negative forces sucking the life out of her. We might even be able to bring John back to our side." Jr. stated with great force, "If I get my hands on John, I'll kick the living snail snot out of him." "Jr., settle down," Bridgett gently scolded. The Professor explained, "If you can't control your emotions anymore than that boy, you're not going to be much good to us or Marilla. Any negative thinking just contributes to Marilla's demise and gives John and those demon dregs more power. You will not be able to connect with the Divine. So, are you with us or not?" Jr., looking sheepish, answered, "I'll do better, I promise." Melissa walked over to Jr. and gave him a big hug and a kiss on the cheek and said, "I'm so proud of you. I know you're going to be awesome on this mission. You've always been my hero." Jr., now as red as a sunburnt Irishman, relinquished his pride for a greater purpose.

Bridgett suggested they all get a good night sleep and continue with the marathon initiation first thing in the morning. "There are pillows and blankets in the living room for everyone, grab yourselves a spot and get comfortable. Professor, I hope your back is up for this." The professor gave Bridgett the thumbs up and picked a large tufted chair to plop into for the night. The professor's pride would never let Bridgett know that his back was already screaming objections to the contorted positions it must endure to fit in that chair.

Arron carefully perused the room for the most befitting spot to accommodate his personal needs: Proximity to the bathroom, clearest path to the kitchen, and furthest distance away from the Professor, in case he snores. Arron took his turn in the bathroom to change into his crisply starched pajamas and perform his meticulous hygiene routine before settling in for the night. A pallet of blankets, precisely positioned on the living room floor, customized to fit the length of Arron's body, awaited the return of its designer. Arron, now ready for bed, said goodnight to his roommate, the Professor. The Professor, with his limbs scattered in every direction relative to the chair, twisted his neck around and painfully replied, "Good night Arron."

Melissa felt electrified, anticipating tomorrow's training session. She climbed into a warm tub of bubbles and soaked herself into a relaxed state, thanking the water for its soothing contribution into tranquility. She whispered words of gratitude into the atmosphere for choosing her to help with the great mission ahead. She asked that Divine guidance and protection be given to the group. With fingers and toes at maximum wrinkle capacity, Melissa said her amens and decided to get out of the tub and ready herself for bed. A pair of flannel pajama pants with matching top lay on the counter waiting to be filled with Melissa's body. Tiny lavender flowers dotted pale yellow material with a lavender bow at the neck line. A perfect nocturnal ensemble for any little princess. Melissa tossed a yellow terry cloth robe over her shoulders, slid her feet into lavender terry slippers, and headed for the living room. She picked the large tufted chair next to the professor to curl up into. She indulged in the fresh clean smell of the comforter Bridgett left for her to use. Melissa took one last sniff of freshness and drifted off to sleep.

Bridgett made her nightly maternal security rounds to make sure all was well before retiring for the night. She scanned the living room, tucking in its inhabitants, and climbed the stairs to Jr.'s room. Jr., already in a deep sleep, received his customary mom hug. The only thing that could wake him now would be the smell of Bridgett's home cooking wafting through the air. Lights out and safe voyaging for this meager league of champions.

CHAPTER 8

RECON

THE SEEDING

*T*HE TEAM QUICKLY TRAVERSED through the energetic veil while their awareness congealed to a clear understanding of their new surroundings, the now parched pacific island of Marilla. Barren of color and leached of its beauty, the island longed for the luster it once emanated. Marilla, the island, and the sea, received the dream team with great need and gratitude, for without intervention, their demise was imminent. "What happened to the island?", Asked Arron. "Never mind the island. What happened to the sea?" Melissa pointed to the murky filth that took the place of the once pristine sea. Jr. gasped, "There's nothing left of it! Where did all the water go?" Bridgett answered, "I'm afraid the evil ones have been working overtime to drain the life from the island, Marilla, and the sea. Let's take a look around the island to locate energy pockets, guides, and defense grids to help us tool up for the battle. The initiates, dazed and befuddled, did not have a clue as to what a guide, grid, or energy pocket is, let alone try to locate one.

The Professor asked the group to huddle up. "Let's make this short and sweet. Clear your mind and relax your body. Put your little Lilliputian feelers out. Walk around the island until you feel a marked difference in the way your body responds to the atmosphere, most likely that will be an energy pocket or defense grid. If you start getting the creeps, go the other way. Animals do this all the time. Bridgett, you take Jr. and Melissa. I'll take Arron. Everyone meet back at this huge grey rock in about a half hour. Go!"

The group split up and stealthily pursued their mark. Arron looked at the professor with amusement, trying to hold down the hysterical laughter ready to bust out of his gut. The professor was in a crouched position, resembling a maimed tiger desperately hunting down his dinner. Arron couldn't decide weather the Professor's back went out on him or he just plum lost his mind. "You're clomping around like Frankenstein boy. Pick up your feet. Pretend you're a jungle cat stalking its prey, skillfully placing your body into the next exquisitely executed position, gently settling your stride into the earth, sensing the soil before your foot is placed, as not to disturb its natural arrangement. Feel the electric charge in the air gently rubbing your skin. Listen for the silence between the sounds of the environment." Arron rolled his eyes and hoped for the best while reluctantly following the Professor.

Bridgett, Jr., and Melissa turned up their senses and tuned into their environment. In silence, they walked the barren island grounds. Jr. felt the hair on his neck and arms rise, as he walked by a large moss covered rock that scantily trickled clean, untarnished water. It was a surprise to see any water left unspoiled by the darkness. He ran to get his mother and Melissa to show them his findings. "Mom, Mel, come quick, I think I found something!" Bridgett and Melissa quickly responded to Jr's excitement and joined him at the mossy rock water fountain. Bridgett closed her eyes and hovered her hands above the water trickle. She felt a clean electric effervescence emanating from the rock. Bridgett gave an enthusiastic nod, acknowledging they hit the jack pot. "Jr., this is exactly what we're looking for. This shows us there is still pure energetic life left on the island. We can build upon this energy to bring back the sea, the island, and Marilla. The Professor will be pleased."

The two scouting parties met back at the rendezvous point. The Professor glowered personal disappointment through his cranky demeanor. All the painstaking stalking the professor demonstrated gleaned an empty harvest. Arron exhaled a half hours worth of time spent with professor grumps, ever so glad to be back with the pack. Bridgett walked over to the professor and gave him a gentle hug. "None of us would be here assisting in this life saving mission if it wasn't for your expertise Professor." The Professor's expression softened while glowing a deep crimson tone, he cleared his throat and said, "You always had a way with me my dear. Somehow, no matter how out of sorts I am, you always bring me back to center." Bridgett started telling the professor about their findings. "I want to show you the pure water source Jr. found here on the island. You will be pleased Professor." So, like a mother goose marching her goslings in single file, Bridgett steered the gaggle towards the golden egg.

Before reaching the mossy water rock, Melissa spotted a cave ahead of them. In her excitement, she ran ahead of the group to explore the cave and the amethyst mist hovering around its mouth. "Mel, wait for us," Jr. hollered out, as he ran to catch up with her. Arron followed right behind Jr., as not to miss a single finding. Bridgett and the professor sauntered behind, eventually meeting up with the exuberant children. The Professor was huffing and puffing between grumbling and cussing, too stubborn to admit he had a hard time keeping up with the children, especially in front of Bridgett. Bridgett was too kind to let the professor know she stayed behind to make sure he didn't pass out before he got to the cave.

The mist at the mouth of the cave hit the group like a brick wall, rapidly seeping into their pores resulting in a kind of euphoric dizziness. Their bodies suddenly received a flush of electric current, charging every body system to full capacity within seconds. "It feels like I drank five pots of coffee, only I don't have the jitters," said Bridgett. The Professor replied, "I feel great. I'm not out of breath and I see everything perfectly clear without my spectacles." The kids laughed till they cried then laughed some more. "What is happening?", Arron asked. The Professor answered, "I'm not sure, let's see if we can muster the gumption to explore further."

As the team ventured further into the cave, an overwhelming sense of peace and compassion filled their hearts. "Do you feel that?", asked Melissa. The Professor agreed, "I haven't felt like this in years. I hope I don't turn into a dad-blame blubbering lovey-dovey." Bridgett smiled and bantered, "I don't think you have anything to worry about Professor, you'll always be that surly old cowboy we all love and respect." The children nodded in agreement. "Let's move on, shall we?" the Professor grumbled.

Melissa fell in love with the magnificent amethyst smoke that floated gracefully in the air. It seemed to form into shapes of angelic beings beckoning her to move deeper into the belly of the cave. "Come on guys, hurry, there is something most heavenly just ahead. When we get back, I need to sketch out a clothing design with this color. Isn't it divine? I feel so inspired."

When the group caught up with Melissa, they found her standing motionless, as if suspended in time, her attention fixated on the cave wall in front of her. They turned to see what she was so captivated by. The entire group stood in a deep freeze, unwilling to turn their gaze away from the celestial being petrified in a chamber of amethyst. The towering angelic form, hibernating in a semi precious casing, stood motionless at a good twelve feet tall. Alabaster wings gracefully curved around a massively muscular body resembling a translucent cocoon. Long, luminous, silver locks of hair trailed over his well developed shoulders. Melissa swooned, swaying in a dreamy trance, "Oh my God, he's gorgeous." "Mel, snap out of it, he's not that gorgeous," Jr. responded. Bridgett replied in a low whisper, "Oh yes he is." "Mom!", Jr. protested.

An amethyst electric wave, pulsating in progressively widening rings, emanated from the face of the wall surrounding the magnificent being. "looks like an angel. What is it doing here?", asked Arron. The Professor and Bridgett looked at each other with astonishment. Bridgett did her best to explain, "I believe this is the guide we've been looking for. It appears this beautiful creature is recharging its battery, so to speak. Do you see the purple pulsating rings? If you close your eyes, you will feel a current of energy rhythmically passing through your body. The amethyst is the charging mechanism." Arron asked, "Do we try to get him out of there, or just communicate with him still stuck in there?"

The Professor asked everyone to gather together and place their hands on the face of the amethyst enclosure. "We need to be precise about this; we all need to focus on a humble request for assistance from this angelic creature. We will say together, nine times: We humbly request your loving guidance in saving our planet from extinction. Help us restore peace, love, and joy into the hearts of mankind." With intense focus, the group repeated their request as instructed.

A resonant, low pitched, pulsating tone emanated from within the amethyst enclosure; breaking the case apart. A sweet smelling liquid burst forth onto the floor of the cave. "Mm, smells like roses," Melissa said. The group stood steadfast and allowed the aromatic nectar to inundate their senses and permeate their pores. Once again, an euphoric feeling of peace, love, and compassion overwhelmed their being.

The divine creature exuded a golden aura, as he stepped out of his cocoon. He stretched his wings, indulging in the unfettered freedom of expansion. As he settled into his newly acquired liberty, he took inventory of the cave dwelling and its occupants. His gaze settled onto the mesmerized group standing in front of him. "What is it you desire of me?" The Professor gathered his faculties to express their urgent need for guidance and assistance. He explained the condition of the island and Marilla, as well as the malevolent plans the sea creatures were bringing to fruition. "I would respectfully address you by name, but I do not know what it is. The earth and all that is innocent is in jeopardy; we need your help. Will you guide us safely through this mission?

The angelic creature took the liberty of moving his wings about in graceful, unhurried undulations, before addressing his audience.

"The time is long since my wings joined the air in dance. Let me take a moment to get re-acquainted with the properties of this space." The divine guide sighed with soothing tones of relaxation, as if settling into a hot bath after a hard days work. "Ahhhh yes, now I remember how wonderful it is to join with the elements. Thank you for moving me from dormancy to the passion of movement."

"My name is Zachriel, you can call me Zach. I will assist you in your struggle to restore harmony on this planet. I am familiar with the battle over the dominance of mind; and how mankind will exploit the vulnerability of innocence."

"In the time of the first millennium, a battle much like the one you now are facing, brought forth armies of my kind to your planet. We came to stimulate the advancement of your spiritual evolution. Hatred, greed, anger, rage, jealousy, and fear ruled your world. There was no honor, no respect for life, no truth in your ways. Humans separated themselves from all that is and ranked themselves above all things. They consumed the gifts entrusted to them without respect, or a paltry speck of gratitude. The gluttonous sacrifice of many pure beings took place for the mere pleasure of their deaths; or to stuff their already obese bellies to a superfluous satisfaction."

"The winged army of light beings did not succeed in bringing the humans to an understanding of the oneness shared with all things. Barbaric thoughts and actions ruled the earth. Some of the winged ones, including myself, where taken hostage and brutalized for monetary gain by selling off bits and pieces of our bodies as charms and souvenirs. Exalted light beings poured forth from the heavens and delivered us from our captors. Some of us, like myself, were left on earth in a pristine location of power to heal our wounds from the battle. We remained in a suspended state until called upon for assistance in times of dire need. Your request for assistance must be of extreme urgency in order to be able to break the healing chamber open."

THE SEEDING

"Have you found any life at all left on this island?", asked Zach. Jr. jumped to the inquiry, "Yes, there is a small trickle of purified water running down one of the rocks we found on the island." Zachriel smiled and let out a breath of relief and said, "good, this will make things a little easier for us. We can build upon the untarnished qualities in the water. Can you get it and bring it to me now?" Jr. enthusiastically jumped at the chance to help. "I'll be back in a jiffy with the goods."

Jr. put his feet in overdrive and made a mad dash for the water. Upon arrival, Jr. realized he needed something to carry the water back with. He put out his feelers and tuned into the resources available to him; meticulously scanning his surroundings for a makeshift receptacle. His eyes finally settled on a hollowed out tree limb laying on the ground a couple feet ahead of him. In his haste to collect his prize, Jr. did not see that someone else shared the desire to posses the prized liquid. A size nine foot slammed down on the tree limb Jr. had his hands on. He looked up and saw John's sardonic smile challenging him to try and take the limb out from under his foot. "I'm not in the mood for your weirdness Parker. Get your foot off now!", Jr. demanded. John Parker, unyielding to Jr's demands, took a swing at his head. Jr. skillfully dodged the intended blow and yanked the limb out from under Johns foot, bringing him to the ground and knocking the wind out of him. Before John could get his bearings, Jr. ladled some water up and beat feet back to the safety of the cave.

Jr. rushed into the cave huffing, puffing, and dripping with perspiration. "I ran into John, our favorite student. He had other plans for our water, but I figured our plans trumped his, so I knocked him on his butt and grabbed what I could; felt real good doin' it too. Hope I got enough to do the job." Jr. held the wooden ladle out for the group to inspect. Zachriel smiled and gave his approval to the measure of water retrieved by Jr. "Leave the precious liquid here with me. I will respectfully excite the archetypal elements from which it was formed and bridge the space between them. This will enable the recognition of their commonality and potentiate their bonding properties."

Zachriel instructed, "It is time for all of you to go into a deeper state of sleep to build up your energy for tomorrow's battle. While you are in the darkness of sleep, I will infuse all of you with a common dynamic vitality and a deeper understanding of the oneness all things share. When you awaken, you will all feel refreshed and become consciously aware of the gifts that were given to you. When we meet again, the precious liquid will have already begun its regeneration process. We will form one creative mind, activating the field to comply with the greater good and restore balance to the earth and it's elements. Your world will be fertile and proliferate a lush bounty once again. So go now and sleep…sleep."

CHAPTER 9

THE FINAL PREPARATION

MICKI EVRIS

*T*HE GROUP DID AS instructed by Zachriel and slept deeper than they ever had before. Bridgett was the first one to get up and greet the new day. "Jr., get up and wake the others for breakfast. We have a lot of ground to cover before tonight, so let's get everyone fueled and ready to rock and roll." "Ok Mom." Jr. did his usual morning ritual: airborne out of the bed landing directly into his pants that rested on the floor from yesterday, splash two drops of water on the face, then down the stairs without touching any. "Mmm, whatcha making Mom? Smells fantabulous!" Bridgett smiled and instructed, "Never mind, just get the others up and in here to eat breakfast."

Jr. snatched a single lavender rose from the vase sitting in the center of the kitchen table and headed for the living room. He stealthily worked his way to Melissa's roosting space, kneeled next to her, and twirled the rose under her nose. Melissa slowly opened her eyes, adjusting her morning blurriness to better define her surroundings. "Jr., you know how much I love lavender, you're a doll, thank you." Jr. put on a gigantic smile and gave Melissa a quick peck on the cheek. "Mom wants us all in the kitchen for breakfast ASAP. Help me get the others up."

Jr. snuck up on the Professors contorted figure and bellowed out a fabricated sneeze. The Professor tumbled out of the chair he was attached to and landed hard on the floor with a bang and a groan. "What in tarnation are you doing boy? Just take me now Lord and deliver me from this juvenile infested, half whited Lilliputian pit of hell." All three children ran over to help peel the Professor off the floor. "You sure made one heck of a thud when you hit the floor professor," Jr. teased. The Professor glowered at Jr. and retorted, "don't push it boy!"

"What's going on in there?", Bridgett hollered from the kitchen. "Breakfast is ready, come in the kitchen and eat before it gets cold." Jr. dropped the Professor like a hot potato which landed him right back on the floor again. "Oh my God, does that boy think of anything else but food?", stated Melissa. Melissa and Arron picked the Professor up off the floor again, having to endure his retributions.

The group assembled in the kitchen, as Bridgett requested. "Jr. stop eating and wait for everyone else to be seated! Where are your manners?", Bridgett scolded. "Sorry Mom, you know I can't resist your raspberry scones," Jr. said as he took one last bite before putting his food down. Everyone ogled the breakfast feast spread out in front of them tantalizing their taste buds: french toast casserole, raspberry scones, broccoli and bacon quiche, apricot muffins, blueberry-sour cream pancakes, and fresh squeezed orange juice. "Would you mind if I take a doggie bag home containing a little of everything? I think I just died and went to heaven. I know I'm in the presence of an angel," the Professor said with great appreciation as he slowly indulged his palate with the delicious zest of an apricot muffin.

"What's on the agenda for today?", Jr. asked as he shoveled another piece of quiche in his mouth. "Don't talk with your mouth full Jr." Bridgett admonished. "Sorry Mom, I'm just getting nervous about tonight. You know how I eat when I get nervous." "You can't possibly eat anymore than you already do!", Melissa expressed with great astonishment. "Let's give the boy a break this time. I have to admit, I'm a little apprehensive about tonight myself and who can resist this splendiferous breakfast," the Professor said. "This is most superb Mrs. Fishman. Can you give my mom some of your recipes?", Arron expressed with great delight. "I'm happy you all find breakfast so appealing. I thought we all deserve a good breakfast before our encounter with the dark side," Bridgett said. The group finished breakfast in silence in order to appreciate every tidbit of culinary delight; the only break in the silence was the sound of smacking lips and mmmms of appreciation.

The group gathered on the back porch after finishing breakfast. "I thought it would be more of a calming atmosphere outside. We could use a little help from natures good vibrations," Bridgett said. Arron opened his notebook and sat poised with pen in hand. "What on earth are you doing boy?", the Professor asked Arron. "I don't want to forget anything. I thought I would review the plan of action before I go to bed tonight," Arron proudly stated. The Professor instructed, "put that down. It's time to relax and absorb the guiding energies of the universe. From now on everything we do will be in a relaxed state and with a unified purpose. Remember the lesson on clearing your thoughts? Well, that's just what we are going to do right now. Let's just sit in silence till those random thoughts show up. I want you to be aware of anything that pops into your brain, examine its origins, and determine if it is beneficial. You will find that ninety-nine percent of those thoughts are useless and not serving any beneficial purpose; clear them."

After a good half hour of thought clearing, the Professor moved to the next phase. "From now on be vigilant in identifying those random thoughts and clear them as soon as possible. Now, as a group, we will direct our attention to connecting with the feeling of unconditional love. As outside thoughts come in, just relax and let them flow right through you. Keep your focus on the feeling of love. Eventually we won't feel the restrictions of our bodies and we will become a single free floating unit in a sea of loving energy. At the point of our united indivisibility, we must draw into our unified self as much pure energy as possible and store it in the eye of our collective consciousness."

The group did as instructed and kept their focus steadfast on the simple singular purpose of gathering loving energy. They felt an effervescent transparency transform the density of their material bodies, followed by a complete dissipation of their ego into a vast sea of nothingness. Diamond bolts of primal activity formed into a vortex of Divine light giving birth to virginal creative potential. The synergic mind of the collective body, apprised with the knowledge of creativity, is now armed and ready for the battle ahead of them. After two hours of gathering and storing creative energy, the group began stepping down from their seamless alliance with the cosmos into the separate dualities of the third dimension. This explosive recognition of the density in their surroundings and the sudden containment of their individuality is suggestive of the forceful spasmodic contractions in the birth canal and umbilical cutting between mother and child.

"Wow, I feel like I've been shot out of a cannon!", Jr. said. The whole group laughed and nodded in agreement. "Can we eat now?", Jr. asked. A simultaneous sigh from the group rang in the air. "I have to admit, I'm pretty hungry myself after that experience. Would you mind my dear Bridgett?", asked Professor Spalding. "I think there is enough leftovers from this morning to have a quick snack," said Bridgett.

"What's the matter Arron? You look stupefied. Did you leave some of your parts behind?", asked the Professor. Arron explained his dilemma, "Well, you know how I like everything to be proven safe, verifiably trusted, organized, and categorized before I let myself anywhere near it? Well, what we just experienced was the exact opposite. It was completely chaotic, without structure, and had no degree of familiarity for me to trust. The funny thing is, I'm ok with it. I feel at peace and full of love. I'm having a hard time making sense if it. How can I feel so good about something that makes no sense and has no definable form for me to identify with? Am I losing my mind?" The Professor smiled and explained, "You now have within you the ability to assign a form to that creative energy force. You, along with the rest of us, will bring order and structure to the chaos with our collective intent. This cosmic stuff is what we will use to bring back the island, Marilla, the sea, and so on. You feel good because our intent was to gather a peaceful, loving energy into our collective field. Does that clarify things for you Arron?" "I think so. Thanks Professor."

The Professor addressed the group, "We are down to that final hour, now here is the plan; We need to get our energy stoked for tonight, so we are going to take an early nap this afternoon with no focus on dream traveling. I'm going to the hammock in the back yard to stretch out and give my aching back a break. I encourage all of you to get as much rest as possible. When we get up, we will convene under the willow tree in the back yard. Bring pillows and blankets. We will dream travel as a collective mind, with a precise, unified purpose; to excite the field with peace, love, and joy. We cannot deviate for one second on the clarity of our purpose. The opposing forces will be amplified as a reciprocal reaction to our positive action. If we continue to stand strong in our purpose, the beauty and grace of the Divine will prevail. Then Jr., we can come back and eat to celebrate our victory. "My mouth is watering already," said Jr.

The group did as instructed and took a good afternoon nap to gather their strength for the battle ahead of them. It was four p.m. before Mrs. Fishman got the children up for a light dinner. "Go wake up the Professor and let him know dinner is ready," instructed Bridgett. The three children went together to get the Professor. "Shhhh, let's spook the poop out of the professor," Jr. playfully suggested. Melissa smiled at Jr. and replied, "You are rotten to the core Jr Fishman." Arron nodded in agreement. Barely maintaining control of their amusement, the children tip-toed across the yard to give the Professor one last Lilliputian pestering before settling down to more serious matters. Now hovering over the peacefully resting professor, at the count of three, all three pranksters let out blood curdling screams, initiating a spin cycle to the professor's hammock before landing him on the ground. "What in tarnation are you three cursed, maladjusted, venomous, banes of my existence trying to do, give me a heart attack?", the professor grumbled as he put his hands to his back to assist in pushing it back into a straightened position. "Mom wants us to come in the house for dinner," Jr. said with a satisfied look on his face. "Boy when this is over, there will be karma to pay," the Professor said as he headed for the house, still rubbing his aching back.

"What do we have here?", asked the Professor as he ogled the contents of the dinner table: Pimento cheese grits, brown butter mashed potatoes, pancetta-wrapped turkey, and Rosemary-black pepper dinner rolls. "My lucky stars! Bridgett, you've done it again, you stole my heart," the Professor said as he quickly found a seat at the table. The children wasted no time finding their way to a spot at the table. "I am most grateful for being a part of this team as well as getting to eat the best food ever in my life," Arran expressed with gratitude. "Mom, you're awesome," Jr. said. "Melissa helped me with this evenings dinner," said Bridgett. "That's my girls!", Jr. proudly stated. "You're a lucky man," said the Professor.

Everyone devoured their dinner indulging in pure culinary ecstasy. They all wished the evenings perfection could last forever. No one would say, but anticipation hung heavy in the air. The time to put their training to the test had finally arrived. "I'll clean the dishes later. I think we better head for the back yard. I've laid out your pillows and blankets in the living room," Bridgett said. Everyone picked out their dream pallets and slowly headed for the willow tree in the back yard. "I'm a nervous wreck and I think I have to pee," Arron said. Jr. and Melissa nodded in agreement. The Professor explained, "It's ok to be nervous, but don't grab a hold of it. Let it ride the air current that flows through you. Feel the peace that is bestowed upon you in every breath you take. Stay focused." "Did you have to use the word flow? Now I really have to pee!", Arron said. Melissa and Jr. agreed. "Well don't just stand there like an Italian cherub in a water fountain, go pee!", the Professor ordered. The children took care of business then quickly resumed their position of repose on their dream pallets.

    The Professor wasted no time leading the group into dream time. "Let's place our pallets closer together so we can join in a circle. Hold the hand of the person on each side of you. This will complete a dynamic energy circuit. Now, as you drift into a theta state, feel a current of peace and love carry you off into deep space. Continue to breathe this bliss into your lungs and then into every part of your being. Maintain this process with impeccable focus till we meet on the other side.

CHAPTER 10

THE BATTLE

WITHIN THE HOUR, THE island received its defenders. Crossing over was a piece of cake for the group. The Professor took charge. "Let's get to the cave and find Zach." As they made their way to the cave, a void of animation and luster on the face of the island became increasingly apparent reminding them of the great urgency required of them to complete their task. As they approached the cave, they could hear muted tones of a furious wind seeking prey to enslave in its whirl. A blanket of misted moss covered the rocks surrounding the gales lair. "It appears Zach was successful in the propagation of our water, look at the moss," Arron said. The group reluctantly moved forward to witness the spectacle. The further they ventured into the depths of the cave, the harder it became to hold their footing. A tunnel of wind captured the gravity of any object insufficiently anchored to the ground and swiftly digested its captives. Bridgett and the Professor quickly corralled the children together to prevent them from being sucked into the belly of the cave. They moved forward as a huddled mass to gain control of their position. Finally a place of peace in the eye of the storm is reached.

The group stood witness to a beautiful angelic figure hovering about two feet above the cave floor. A torrent of pure water swirled around Zach's magnificent form. The original ladle of pure water lie cradled in Zach's hands. Acting as a conduit between the ethers and the ladled water, Zach drew the archetypal elements from ethereal space and forged a copulative affect between those primal elements and the water, giving birth to the new liquid life now swirling around him. The whirlwind gradually mellowed into a gentle sprinkle as a rich voluminous waterfall began to flow from the rocks at the side of the cave. A river formed to carry the new born water out to the sea.

Zach's hovering form slowly touched down onto the cave floor as he regained awareness of his surroundings. "I am pleased to see you all made it back for the final battle. While you slumbered safely in your beds, I have programmed your subconscious minds to identify the voice of my guidance when needed. You may receive intuitive flashes guiding you to respond in a way that is out of your comfort zone or out of character for you. If you panic, you will not be in a position to receive this guidance. Are you ready to begin?" The group demurely expressed their readiness to proceed.

Zach instructed, "Gather at the edge of the sea and call upon the three beasts: Plio, Mosas, and X. You must employ the use of great authority in your words and demand they show the true face of their nature. Forge the instrument of victory with the reciprocal of their negative intent. When they thrust anger, counter with joy. When they instill fear, stand courageous. A beautifully cultivated core will break through the barren crust of hatred to bear the fruit of victory. If you remain impeccably focussed on your task, you will be the champions of a lush and prosperous future. The slightest break in confidence will be detected by your enemy, leaving your tender side vulnerable for attack. If you are defeated, your world will no longer be. Remember, I will always be with you to assist in guidance and protection. I will keep the virginal waters flowing through the island to the sea, this will dilute the force of our opposition. Go now and let the elements of the Divine flow through you."

The group gathered at the waters edge as instructed. "Join hands and become one with me," instructed the Professor. The Professor looked out towards the sea and shouted with great command,

"Come Plio, come Mosas, come X, come to me
show your true nature you've woven you three
come on, come come on, come give it your all

> for the power of one will fight till you fall
> Innocence rises to burn your disease
> laughter and joy brings you down to your knees
> now the sea rises with liquid divine
> to nurture the life you took from the brine
> surrounded by life giving virtue are thee
> so come on, come come on, come forth you dark three"

Three large bubbling circles formed at the edge of the sea. The vapors rising from the churning water brought forth a repulsive stench erupting into a corrosive fog temporarily blinding its opposition. Arron's lungs protested with a series of convulsive barks as he painfully expressed, "It feels like I just inhaled pure acid. I can't breathe." Clasping at their throats and rubbing their bleeding eyes, the group fell to their knees feeling defeated before the battle started. Jr. choked out a plea for help, "What do we do now Professor?" The Professor painfully replied, "Get back in a circle quickly before they rise from the water. I know it's hard but you must push forward." The group did as the professor asked and wormed their way towards each other. "Mel, grab my hand and I'll help you," Jr. said, as he reached forward to aid his dearest love. The Professor grabbed Arron and Bridgett and helped the group back into a circle. The Professor instructed, "Now become one in the desire to bring forth beauty, love, and compassion to the earth. This desire is more powerful than you realize, especially when we do it in synchronicity. This is what we trained for. Block out all the pain, fear, and especially doubt and focus your little Lilliputian brains as hard as you can on the task at hand. I need you to listen to my voice and nothing else. Fill your entire being with the sound of each word. Feel the words vibrate within your body. The Professor chanted, "I am loved. I am grateful. I am filled with peace and beauty." The group chanted with the Professor until their voices chimed as one sacred bell.

THE SEEDING

A sweet smelling rain poured forth and washed the blood from their eyes and a fresh mist cleared the pain from their lungs. Their focus, now effortless, formed a protective barrier around them. The corrosive vapors, now neutralized, dissipated into the pure waters of the sea.

Plio, Mosas, and X rose from the sea, throwing their bodies to and fro in an angry rage, casting off the fresh formed mist that glistened on their undeserving bodies. John Parker riding on the neck of X, shot a disdainful glare at Jr. and shouted, "What are you doing Fishman, trying to defeat these three? I see you brought that group of impotent fools with you. Give it up, you'll never defeat us. You think a little rain sprinkle can weaken our power? I think not." X reared up from the depths of the water and bellowed out a thunderous roar, creating a tidal wave of fury.

The roars of X could not break through the protective barrier surrounding the group. he tried, and tried again before retreating back to his position in the sea. All three sea demons rose up together and slammed their bodies hard against the water creating a tsunami of rage, all of which washed over the group leaving them untouched. John mocked, "Do you plan on spending the rest of your lives in that stupid huddle or are you gonna fight back?"

Jr. broke away from the circle and lunged towards John and X. "That's it Parker, I've had it with you, get off that giant slug and fight like a man!" X flung his body hard on the ground, just missing Jr., leaving a mammoth fissure behind as a reminder of the destruction he is capable of. Jr., unshaken by the power of X, sprang to his feet and challenged John Parker once again. "Are you gonna let X do all your dirty work for you Parker, or are you man enough to come down here and fight?"

X arched his neck towards the ground to let John Parker climb off. "You think you can take me Fishman? Come on, your rage is what I live for." As soon as Jr. heard Johns words, he realized he was stoking the fires of hell by reacting to Johns provocations. Jr. backed away from John and rejoined his companions. "You almost had me there Parker. Thanks for the lesson in how to defeat your enemy."

John rushed forward and plunged his body forcefully into the group to break them apart. He grabbed Melissa's hair and yanked it hard enough to pull her off the ground. She was barely balancing on the tips of her toes. Melissa let out a painful scream. John covered her mouth with his hand to quiet her before forcing his lips upon hers to steal a kiss. Jr. couldn't contain his rage anymore, especially when it came to Melissa. He charged forward to take a swing at Parker, stumbling to the ground as he missed his mark. "Now that's more like it. I love it when you're down, defeated, and full of piss and vinegar," Parker hissed.

Jr. regained his composure, picked himself up off the ground and slowly walked towards Parker. "What are you going to do Jr., love me to death?", Parker sarcastically bated Jr. Jr. realized that what Parker said made sense. John thrives on fear, hate, anger, and negative thoughts. Love would be the best weapon to defeat him. Jr. reached deep inside his mind and called upon Zachriel for help. A purple mist wrapped around Jr.'s body, seeping into every pore. Jr. glowed with an angelic beauty that grew brighter with every positive thought. He walked towards Parker, gaining confidence with each step. John averted his gaze away from Jr. His eyes burned from the intensity of the light. John released the grip he had on Melissa to cover his face, leaving Melissa free to run.

John Parker scurried back to his place of power, riding on the neck of X, to retaliate before Jr. and the group could regain focus. X lunged forward in fury snapping at Jr. Jr parried the rabid mouth of X and vaulted onto his neck, landing behind Parker. As the two foes exchanged blow for blow, Plio and Mosas surged forward to attack Bridgett, Arron, and Melissa. Arron picked up a softball size rock and positioned himself in front of the two girls. Waiting for the perfect shot, Arron pitched the rock straight down Plio's throat, halting the daemon in his tracks. Bridgett followed Arron's line of action and pitched a rock at Mosas missing the mark by a mile. Mosas took a deep breath and forcefully blew out liquid acid, setting the beach on fire. The group scattered for cover from the flames.

The Professor wailed out a plea towards the heavens for Zachriel to intervene. "ZACHRIEL!!! You have promised guidance to us in times of great need. Now is the time to show the strength of your promise, for without your presence we shall surely perish!"

The Professor silenced his thoughts to clear a space for Zachriels words of guidance. A mighty voice gave clear instruction to the professor, "You must sacrifice yourself for the lives of the innocent. The sea daemons cannot survive in the presence of selfless love. Everything else will fall into a place of restored beauty when the beasts are destroyed."

The Professor took a deep breath and gathered the strength to carry out his fated task. The Professor walked to the waters edge and with great command called for the attention of the sea demons.

"Come Plio, come Mosas, come X, come to me
I give you my life to take down with you three
come on, come come on, come take what you will
take all that I am for your bellies to fill.
Weak and defeated I will fuel your disease
do what you will with my life as you please
roll me down under, roll me down deep
come take my soul, my soul you will keep
Sacrificial lamb, yes yes that is me
so come on, come come on, come forth you dark three."

The pandemonium screeched to a halt as if someone pulled the plug to the motion of chaos. X whipped his neck abruptly to rid himself of the two warring riders perched on the battlefield his neck supplied. Plio and Mosas quickly reset their focus on the professor allowing Bridgett, Arron, and Melissa to run for cover. All three daemons now had their attention steadfast on the Professor.

A look of doubt and mistrust reflected in the beasts expressions with squinted eyes, tilted heads, and jutting tongues. "I taste deception in your breath. Do you mean to give of yourself freely to supply our needs? This is not a common thing a human would do. What is your intent?", Mosas inquired.

The Professor courageously turned his gaze upward towards the beasts and answered, "What part of sacrifice do you not understand? I'm offering you my soul, you simple minded slug! Do I have to open your mouth and jump in?" The Professor no sooner got the words out of his mouth when Plio surged forward and snatched him off the ground. The three sea daemons spasmodically yanked and tugged at the Professor's now limp body till they each took possession of their own piece of the pie.

John raised his fisted hands to the sky and let out a blood curdling screech of victory. "Let this be a lesson to all of you. You will never defeat the mighty three!" X heaved his body forward and devoured his loyal servant John, without thought or hesitation. The horrified companions stood frozen in their tracks, unable to comprehend the vacuum abruptly created with the absence of their respected mentor and their abhorred foe.

An explosion of brilliant gold light rose from the sea and shot up towards the heavens like a Roman candle geyser. As the incandescence settled high into the northern sky, the shape of a serpent formed from the stars created by the blast forming the constellation Draco. The companions looked towards the heavens with bittersweet tears running down their cheeks. The battle is finished with the promise of lush new beginnings at the cost of loosing their friend and mentor, Professor Spalding. "I'm gonna miss that surly old man," Arron said. "Me to," Jr. said.

Melissa nudged Jr. and directed him to look at the waterfall now gushing from the rock cliff behind them. A beautiful liquid female figure rose from the mist and started humming a delightful tune. "Marilla!", Jr. gleefully shouted out. "I thought I would never see you again." Marilla looked down at the weary warriors and beckoned them to come closer. The group found a narrow pathway leading to the top of the cliff, carefully placing one foot directly in front of the other as not to loosen any of the pathway. One misplaced footstep, and it's a long fall down to the rocks below. The closer they got to the top, the sweeter the misty petrichor they experienced with every breath.

As each member of the group topped the cliffs, they were captured by the spell of Marillas alluring gaze. A peaceful euphoria filled the air within and without each weary warriors spirit. Marillas gratitude was expressed by the infusion of her liquid being into the fabric of life itself, uniting all things with a ribbon of fluid energy.

The tension of the battle melted away as each member of the group took a seat on the ground in front of Marilla. The overwhelming sense of unity experienced between the group and Marilla gave birth to a new wisdom. They could feel Marillas fluid body running through their veins and further on through everything around them. A shimmering silver glow permeated all things. All things contain the beauty of Marilla, only needing to be recognized by all things. To recognize the commonality of the shared primal substance we are all fashioned by is to amplify the brilliance of the One. The group drifted into a blissful state of repose transporting them back to their pallets at the Fishman home.

CHAPTER 11

THE HOMECOMING

THE SEEDING

*T*HE SCENT OF BACON wafting through the air caught the immediate attention of Jr. He jumped out of bed in his usual manner and dashed down the stairs to the living room to awaken his companions. "Mel, wake up, we made it home safe and sound. Mom must be making bacon and eggs, I could smell it all the way upstairs, woke me right up." Melissa slowly propped herself up on her elbows to look her handsome hero in the eyes and said, "Jr., you came to wake me up before going to the kitchen. Are you feeling alright?" Jr. looked at his sweeten-treat and affectionately replied, "Mel, you are the most important thing in my life, even more than food, I just want you to know that." Melissa replied, "I think that is the sweetest thing you have ever said to me, and you, Jr. Fishman, mean more to me than lavender." Arron now awake said, "Oh my God, you guys are making me vomit with that loveydovey stuff, stop already!

Bridgett came down the stairs stretching her arms and yawned out her inquiry, "which one of you sweethearts started breakfast?" Jr. looked at his mother and said, "Mom, we didn't start breakfast. If we didn't start breakfast and you didn't start breakfast, then who is making breakfast?" The group all looked at each other in complete astonishment and ran into the kitchen, banging into each other to be the first to gain sight of the cook in question. A hardy masculine voice boomed out the question, "Anyone up for a good belly stuffing this fine morning? I have here the most fantabulistic breakfast in town just waiting to be gobbled up by my favorite daemon slayers." The Professor turned and gave the group a gnarly look with one eye brow cocked higher than the other, the stink eye, as Jr. would call it, and said, "What, are you waiting for me to chew it for you and place it down your gullets like little baby birdies? Get your miserable Lilliputian backsides in here and sit down to eat!" The group rushed forward in a singular clump, with exalted tones simultaneously shouting, "Professor!!!" The Professor didn't have time to dodge the group before they tackled him, inundating him with affection and a flurry of questions to be answered.

A high pitched barking noise came from ground level breaking the groups focus momentarily. "What is this puppy doing in my house?" asked Bridgett. "Mom, can we keep him?" begged Jr. Melissa sighed, "He's the cutest thing ever with his gorgeous blue eyes and grey and white suite coat." Arron added, "I think that's a Husky pup." The Professor explained, "This is Zach. I found him laying in my lap when I woke up in the hammock, in fact he woke me up licking me with that slimy tongue of his. I knew it was Zach when he jumped down from the hammock and bolted for the little rock waterfall that is now in your back yard garden. He looked at me, then back at the waterfall several times before begging me to pick him up. I figure Zach and I will make good roommates, sorry Jr., don't mean to take the wind out of your sail."

"We thought you died Professor! Tell us what happened," queried Bridgett. The Professor smiled and explained, "I thought I was a goner myself when the daemons split me apart and swallowed me up for dinner. When the beasts exploded into the heavens, I was released from the prison in their belly and floated down deep into the sea. Marilla gathered my parts together and called upon the healing spirit of the sea. The passion of Marillas request to salvage my life, together with the compassion of the sea flowing through me, well let's just say it put Humpty Dumpty back together again. I feel clean inside and out now. Marilla told me it was my love for you children that created the explosion of the beasts. For the life of me, I don't know how she figured that. I thought I finally had some peace and quiet without the lot of you hanging around raising a ruckus, making me pull my hair out." The group all rushed towards the Professor, inundating him with hugs and affection till he broke it up with his usual grumbling and complaining, "All right, that's enough! I don't want all those germs you kids seem to carry leaping onto my recently cleaned and renovated body. Let's eat breakfast." "I'm for that!", Jr. chimed in.

The group sat down to a hero's breakfast, exploding with the excitement of their conquest and the return of their mentor, Professor Spalding. Arron asked, "What happened to John? Did you meet him in the belly of the beast?" The Professor explained, "You have to remember, we were traveling into other dimensions. Many alternates of you and many alternate outcomes exist in those dimensions. John is in the belly of the beast in one dimension and home eating bagels and lox in another." Jr. expressed his chagrin, "You mean to tell me we went through all of that for nothing?" The Professor chuckled and explained, "What is accomplished or experienced in one dimension, will have an impact on all the other dimensions. We altered the future pathway the earth and its inhabitants will take. I believe we augmented the vitality of our earth. If She is threatened in the future, She will have more energy to withstand an attack from any type of succubus or human beast. We are now entangled with the earth in a deeper way than before. We are familiar with Her alternate reality, and have forged a beautiful and loving relationship with Her." Bridgett chimed, "Amen to that."

The Professor cleared his throat and stood up to make an important announcement, "I want you children to know that you all passed my class with an A plus. You have mastered inter dimensional travel and can control what happens in your dreams. You have learned to discipline your thoughts and have chosen to project positive waves of energy into the space that joins all things. I am very proud of you. As a matter of fact, I want the three of you to assist, as Bridgett does, in the education of future academy students. You will be considered a part of the faculty. I have some clout in determining who gets picked to assist me. What do you think? Will you join me in this wondrous adventure?" Frozen in the moment, with their mouths agape, the children looked at each other in disbelief. Bridgett and the Professor looked at each other with a smile while waiting for the children to snap out of their stupor. After a long pause, the children all chimed in at once with exuberant heck yea's and wow's. The Professor raised his glass of juice and pronounced a toast, "To the cosmic crusaders!" The group all shouted together, "To the cosmic crusaders!"

A knock on the front door intruded on their salutes. "I'll get it Mom," said Jr. as he dashed from the kitchen to answer the door. "Are you kidding me?", Jr. gasped. The group strained their necks to see past the kitchen archway and get a glimpse of what Jr. was reacting too. "Hi Jr., I thought you might be interested in the likes of this unusual collection, so I wanted to come by and surprise you with it." There, standing in front of Jr. sporting a nefarious smirk, was John, Jr.'s nemesis, holding a small terrarium housing three small lizards. "I found these in my back yard this morning and thought you would be the perfect pal to give them to. I named them Plio, Mosas, and X," John said with a salty edge to his words, as he shoved the glass box into Jr.'s gut. "See you in class tomorrow Jr." John walked away sporting a cocky swagger as he waved goodby to Jr. Jr. looked down at the three lizards in disbelief and bellowed, "Professor, Mom, you're not gonna believe this!!"

EPILOGUE

A READERS
COMPANION TO
THE SEEDING

This is a useful guide for a practical application of the concepts expressed throughout this book. The manifestation of this book is a result of applying these principles. Reposed perseverance is the only requirement needed for success.

Guidance may be received in very soft and subtle ways that can hide behind the mental blathering we inundate ourselves with, that is why the first step is clearing the mind.

The reticular activating system (RAS) is a filter between your conscious and subconscious mind. Affirmations, intentional or unintentional, send a message to the (RAS) to pay attention to the important message it is receiving and store it for future use. It is important to note what message you are telling the (RAS) to hang onto. Becoming aware of your inner chatter, which are affirmations, will give you the freedom to choose what programs to keep or get rid of.

Once you resolve yourself to diligently recognize the words that are rattling around inside your mind, programming your subconscious, you will begin to hear the good, the bad, and the ugly affirmations that are running amuck, influencing the outcomes of your desires. A good place to start is when you take a relaxing bath, where you are not asleep but relaxed enough to start the weeding process. When you are not pre-occupied with the responsibilities of life and are in a relaxed state, stored programs will come to the forefront of your mind. Now you may gather the spoiled seeds planted and gracefully pluck them from your garden. Eventually you will recognize thought intrusions at any given time.

When you become aware of each thought, examine how they make you feel, how they change or influence the way you respond to life situations, and how repetitive they are. This appraisal will give you an idea how far off the beaten path you are from experiencing your life's purpose. Are you living someone else's dream, or programming yourself for failure? Some of these thoughts have been living within you since early childhood and have surfaced, giving you an opportunity to acknowledge them and send them into space to dissipate. Eventually, you realize that all you have to do is not react to them and let them flow through you, but first they must be recognized as an existing influence.

In chapter 10, Jr. learns that he can gain the upper hand in a battle with John Parker by not reacting to his provocations. Once you react to something, you will be tied to it in many ways:

1) Entrainment is a type of shared reaction that synchronizes your energy to a collective action.

2) Entanglement links reactions, through time and space; to anyone you have ever come in contact with.

3) Energy cords link you to the thing you are reacting to and will amplify the effects.

4) Affirmations anchor the reaction, influencing your future actions.

Learning not to react can be somewhat of a challenge. One of the ways I have found to be effective goes like this: you catch a fleeting thought that, upon examination, makes you tense, sad, or irritable. To begin rectification, imagine your body to be transparent, and a calm liquid force is flowing through you. The tension, sadness, and irritability dissipates into the current and flows out into the environment outside of your body. Be aware of the calming effect on your body as you are relieving the negative influences of your thought programs. Know that when nothing matters, nothing can attach itself to you, including thought programs, and you are free to receive what you truly need. When I say nothing matters, I mean everything has the same neutral strength or importance. Nothing is defined as good or bad. No dichotomy is created to make a judgement over. Only let momentum gather when you have the ability to let go of that accumulated energy, good or bad. Superfluous energy accumulation robs your entire being of smooth, frictionless flow and will eventually create disease or pain.

Continue to acknowledge your inner chatter and float those thoughts and reactions out into space. This will become a part of your everyday routine. Soon you will be able to process those intrusions lickity-split. Make sure you feel gratitude, inside and out, for completing the clearing process. No matter how small your steps, acknowledge your progress.

After your mind is clear, it will be easier to receive the benefits from meditation. The first step in meditation, as you might have guessed, is to relax all the tension in your body. This can be done using a variety of methods. One of my favorite ways to relax my body goes something like this: Without using any accessory muscles, take long, deep breaths. Feel the air, filled with tiny particles of peace, inundate your body as you breathe. Feel these particles effortlessly flow in and out like a wave, taking the tension with it as it leaves with the exhale. Gradually let your breathing go back into a normal rhythm. If any intruding thoughts come forward, let them ride the peace wave out into the atmosphere. If you notice any painful or tight areas in your body, let them merge with the particles of peace and gently float outside your body. Don't label the things you feel with names like: I feel pain, sadness, fear, etc. These labels will only define those feelings and imbed them deeper.

Once you feel relaxed, present any questions you may have to the universal space surrounding you before going any deeper. Try to stay unattached and neutral when asking your question. Let yourself drift into the deep space that is filled with a peaceful knowing. Be delicately aware of pictures, symbols, or phrases that come and go quickly. Don't try and figure it out until you come out of the meditation. Sometimes answers will be given to you days later. Don't expect or demand anything. Feel as if all you need is floating in the midnight space of peace and all is as it should be. When there is no resistance or expectation, you are open to receive the gifts already saturating the space around you. Keep a journal or recording of the mental impressions you receive. It is easier to identify common themes and the meaning of symbols when you journal. Meditations often lead to dreaming.

Dreams can have an effect on your waking life. That is why it is beneficial to control what happens in your dreams. To be actively aware of yourself while you are dreaming is called lucid dreaming.

Before drifting off into a deep sleep, tell yourself to remember your dreams, you might have to do this for a month, give or take. When you remember one or two dreams a week, start telling yourself you will be aware of yourself in your dreams before you slide into a reposed state. Be aware of anything that could not be done normally while you are awake. If you can recognize the strange and extraordinary things in your dreams, you will be aware you are dreaming and be able to actively effect what is happening. Another way to recognize you are dreaming is to look at your hands, or another part of your body. Do not over-focus on anything or you could loose your lucid space.

While in a lucid state, you can redirect a bad dream to be something more appealing. It is possible to rid yourself of nightmares or inner fears. In one of my dreams, my boss was trying to bash my head in with a rock. I was able to change this fear based expression by glaring at my foe and telling him he can't hurt me. When he tried to hit me with the rock, it went right through me. My boss was horrified and went running off into the desert. In real life, I gained more confidence around authority figures.

You might receive a message, warning, or recommendation while in a lucid state. One night I saw a military figure telling a person of a higher rank to terminate my job. I abruptly woke up and figured I better be asking for guidance on this one. I asked for clarification and a solution to be given in a very obvious way. The next day I received my solution in an e-mail from a job I applied for a year prior. The message went like this: "I wanted to let you know if you are not satisfied with your position at your present job, there is one waiting for you here. You just popped into my mind this morning, so I thought I would contact you for the position." This is also a good example of entanglement. A woman I interviewed with once, connected with my desire for a solution. We were still linked on a subtle level and responding to one another.

The military figure was a military nurse. I did not know this nurse was military until I went to work that evening. She was indeed undermining me.

Guidance is there for you, you just have to ask for it, then be aware of subtle cues. The meaning of the message may not be clear to you at first. Let it delicately marinate for a while before trying to determine the essence of the message. I started having an increase in back and knee pain. I asked for help before going to sleep. I heard a voice say, "You have to stop playing the cello." I was upset in hearing this because I love to play the cello. I ended up changing my sitting position while I practiced. I did not need to quit playing. I was pointed in the direction where changes had to be made. The pain diminished dramatically.

Let's talk about how to recognize entrainment, and how to use it to your advantage. Let's say you're at a party where you get sucked into a political debate, just two people pointing out the negatives of the local government. This stirs up all sorts of aggressively fearful emotions. A couple of friends join into the fear fest, then another, and another, and so on. Anger builds and voices raise. A couple guys start pushing each other, then another, and another. The party turns into a brawl, the place gets trashed, and you get arrested with the group. You not only allowed yourself to be negatively entrained, but you reacted to it, creating an amplified energy link, contributing to it's momentum. This is how riots get started.

Have you ever been in a waiting room and noticed the entire staff's general vibe to be sullen and down right rude? All it takes is one bad attitude and the entire staff jumps on board the funk train. Now that you know about entrainment, you don't have to buy into their mood; you might even be able to change the ambiance of the room by using the same concept.

Entrainment can also work with inanimate objects. I had a computer that I had no great love for, every time I tried to use it, it would go off on tangent agendas. My computer had no problem working properly for anyone else but me. My dislike for that computer created a connection to it, entraining a mutual negative response to one another.

Once you become aware that there is such a thing as entrainment, it is easier to stop your involvement with it and avoid the resulting consequences.

As discussed in the prologue, entanglement is when two or more particles interact with each other, irrespective of distance; a correlation will always exist between them. What effects one particle will always effect the other, no matter how far apart they are separated. On a larger scale, as people interact with each other in life, they will remain entangled in one way or another. The twin's effect is a good example of entanglement involving people. There are numerous cases documented involving twins that are separated by great distances that respond to each other's life changing situation. There are also documented cases of animals finding their human companions from thousands of miles away. One woman kept staring at a picture of a cat she lost on a cross country move when he jumped out of the car at a rest stop. The cat walked his way across several states to be reunited with his owner months after their separation. How many times have you received a phone call from someone you had been thinking about? I could give a million examples of similar situations. The point is, "No man is an island", and we are all just a part of the sea.

Our connection to all things is a great responsibility. Just as we can be a victim of another's thoughts, we can also contribute to the peace or distress of a past or present acquaintance. The trick is to keep your thoughts in check and try not to react to an arbitrary thought or happenstance. Whatever you think about will create a link to it. The link creates a cause and effect reaction. We are all responsible for those random thoughts popping into each other's minds.

*Be vigilant in recognizing idle chatter programming your subconscious.

*Try and relax your body as often as possible to be able to recognize when you are reacting to something. A tense body will restrict energy flow, creating an opportunity for disease.

*Controlling your reactions will limit the link you have to what you are reacting to.

*Be on the look out for entrained events happening around you. If possible, remove yourself from the whirlwind of emotions trying to pull you in.

*Respect all things as much as you would respect yourself, after all, the same cosmic stuff runs through all things.

*Get involved in your dreams to overcome personal challenges.

*Remember your thoughts effect more than just you.

*Maintain a loving energy as much as possible.

I look forward to further communications with all of you. Peace, love, and joy be with you always.

ABOUT THE AUTHOR

*M*ICKI RECEIVES HER INSPIRATION from the soul of the Blue Ridge Mountains in Ellijay, Georgia. The quiescent wisdom of the forest conveys a message of the energetic unity all things share, bringing depth to the meditations that are practiced daily.

She offers an occasional serenade to her surroundings with her cello, Bridgett. Her two canine companions, Cleo and Anthony, have kindly offered to share their living space with her.

The jungle kitty, Mojo, prefers to offer bits and pieces of his superior wisdom while perched in his usual elevated position of royalty.

Micki works as an RN in the neighboring town of Dalton. She is a composer, wood carver, and artist, with a special love for Native American art.

Micki is a Guinness world record holder in weightlifting and powerlifting and uses this strength in all her pursuits.

www.ingramcontent.com/pod-product-compliance
Lightning Source LLC
Chambersburg PA
CBHW060407080526
44583CB00012B/499